The Undergraduate's Companion
to English Renaissance Writers
and Their Web Sites

The Undergraduate's Companion to English Renaissance Writers and Their Web Sites

Steven K. Galbraith

Undergraduate Companion Series

LIBRARIES
UNLIMITED
A Member of the Greenwood Publishing Group
Westport, Connecticut • London

Library of Congress Cataloging-in-Publication Data

Galbraith, Steven Kenneth.
  The undergraduate's companion to English Renaissance writers and their web sites / by
    Steven Kenneth Galbraith.
      p. cm. — (Undergraduate companion series)
    Includes bibliographical references and index.
    ISBN 1–59158–140–0
    1. English literature—Early modern, 1500–1700—Computer network resources. 2.
  Authors, English—Early modern, 1500–1700—Biography—Computer network resources. 3.
  Renaissance—England—Computer network resources. I. Title. II. Series.
  PR421.G35 2004
  025.06'8209—dc22   2003060594

British Library Cataloguing in Publication Data is available.

Library of Congress Catalog Card Number: 2003060594
ISBN: 1–59158–140–0

First published in 2004

Libraries Unlimited, 88 Post Road West, Westport, CT 06881
A Member of the Greenwood Publishing Group, Inc.
www.lu.com

Printed in the United States of America

The paper used in this book complies with the
Permanent Paper Standard issued by the National
Information Standards Organization (Z39.48–1984).

10   9   8   7   6   5   4   3   2   1

Love to Jeannie and Bucket.

S.K.G.

Contents

Introduction, or Research in the Early Twenty-First Century

This book, the latest addition to the Undergraduate's Companion series, confirms that the literature of Renaissance England is alive and well in the new millennium. Through more than four centuries, the works of authors such as Edmund Spenser, John Milton, and William Shakespeare have been preserved in the pages of books. With the advent of the Internet, a technological innovation as profound today as the printing press was to early modern England, these authors are once again in the midst of a renaissance. Digitally reborn and no longer confined to static printed pages, they are only a click away from a new generation of readers who may soon find themselves *Surfing with the Bard*.

Renaissance studies are also alive and well in colleges and universities throughout the world. Home to fundamental English authors such William Shakespeare and John Donne, this literary period continues to be a popular and dynamic academic field for students and professors. On one hand, many students of literature begin their study with the English Renaissance – Shakespeare often provides an introduction to drama, and the sonnet is often the starting point for the study of poetry. On the other hand, Renaissance scholars continue to remain on the cutting edge of literary criticism, consistently leading scholarship in exciting new directions. The Internet is no exception. As many of the Web sites listed in this companion demonstrate, Renaissance scholars are adapting well to the digital environment.

Drawing from both the digital environment and the traditional world of print, this companion aims to augment classroom studies and library research by joining these two media into one resource. This fusion is the research environment of the early twenty-first century. The time will come when the majority of good information will be online, but until then the most successful researchers will move fluidly between the worlds of digital and print searching for the best information.

Audience

The *Undergraduate's Companion to English Renaissance Writers and Their Web Sites* is aimed primarily at undergraduates participating in survey courses and in upper-level seminars that engage the literature of the English Renaissance. To meet the needs of these students, this companion includes authors found in recent editions of the *Norton Anthology of British Literature Volume I*, the *Longman Anthology of British Literature Volume I*, and similar anthologies. Beyond this primary audience, the resources included in this companion are flexible enough to address the needs of both graduate and high school students. Moreover, many of the sites may provide teaching resources for professors and instructors.

The Authors

This companion uses as its base the list of authors found in James K. Bracken's *Reference Works in British and American Literature* (Englewood, Colo.: Libraries Unlimited, 1998). For author's names and dates this companion uses *The Oxford Companion to English Literature*, 6th ed. (New York: Oxford University Press, 2000). The English Renaissance is defined as spanning from the late fifteenth century (authors such as John Skelton), to the late seventeenth century (authors such as John Milton and Andrew Marvell). Reflecting current trends in literary criticism and expanding notions of diversity, this volume moves beyond the traditional canon. Writers such as Aemilia Lanyer, Isabella Whitney, and Thomas Dekker sit alongside Shakespeare, Milton, and Spenser. Furthermore, this companion includes writers who are not strictly literary. Important figures in religion and philosophy such as John Foxe, Anne Askew, and Thomas Hobbes have entries, as do major political figures such as Queen Elizabeth I and King James I. Following the methodology of the previous books in this series, each author must be the subject of a quality Web site to be included.

In this companion, authors are arranged alphabetically (a chronological index is also provided in the back of the book). Each author's entry may contain any or all of the following categories: Web Sites; Biographies and Criticism; Dictionaries, Encyclopedias, and Handbooks; Indexes and Concordances; Journals; and Bibliographies. If there are no resources for any of the categories, then that category is omitted.

Web and print citations follow the current *MLA Handbook for Writers of Research Papers* (New York: Modern Language Association of America, 2003), unless they are previously cited in either the "Frequently Cited Web Sites" or "Frequently Cited References," in which case they are slightly abridged.

A Note on Shakespeare

Shakespeare may well be the most popular author in the English language. It should come as no surprise that the number of Shakespeare sites surpasses that of any other author in this companion (or, for that matter, in the entire *Undergraduate's Companion* series). Shakespeare's entry, therefore, is the most robust, containing over eighty Web sites. To help organize this overwhelming amount of information, subentries for each of his works have been added to the standard categories. For example, there are subentries for *Hamlet, Romeo and Juliet, Richard III*, the poems and sonnets, and so forth. There are also subentries for "Dictionaries, Encyclopedias, and Handbooks," such as General Handbooks and Guides; Pronunciation Guides; Quotations and Coinages; and Who's Who.

Web Sites

Despite the help of powerful search engines such as Google and subject-organized directories such as Yahoo!, finding quality information online can sometimes be a difficult task. Finding current information can be even more daunting. In compiling Web resources for this companion, the greatest effort was made to find sites that would be valuable to undergraduate students – sites that offer primary works, biographical information, secondary criticism, and study guides. Every Web site entry in this companion is accompanied by an annotation. Annotations tend to be more descriptive than evaluative. Users may begin with the assumption that the inclusion of a site means it has something valuable to offer. Sites that do not are simply not included.

Print Resources

Whereas digital resources are a relatively new development, print resources for the study of English Renaissance writers have been accumulating for centuries. Understandably, sifting through four hundred years of editions, biographies, bibliographies, and criticism is a task that few students wish to take on. Fortunately, at the heart of this companion's print resources are two series that have already done most of that work. The first, *Literature Criticism from 1400 to 1800* (Detroit: Gale, 1984–), distills centuries of literary criticism into concise yet comprehensive entries that provide excerpts of significant literary criticism. For example, the entry for John Milton in volume 9 of the series contains excerpts of Milton criticism from 1652 through 1988 (155–266). The more frequently studied authors often are given more than one entry in the series; therefore, Milton is updated in volume 34 with excerpts of criticism from 1941 through 1996 (329–427). The second resource is *The Dictionary of Literary Biography* (Detroit: Gale, 1978–). Arranged thematically into individual volumes such as *Elizabethan Dramatists* and *British Philosophers, 1500–1799*, this series provides detailed entries on the life and works of most of the writers included in this companion (see the section "Frequently Cited References" for a list of the volumes used). Building on these two resources, this companion also includes several book series that are useful for undergraduates. For example, volumes in Twayne's English Authors Series provide solid critical introductions to authors, and Macmillan's *Literary Lives Series* produces biographies aimed at undergraduates. Other series include Longman's *Critical Readers* and Garland's *Shakespeare Criticism.*

Using This Companion

Although tremendous progress has been made in publishing valuable information on the Internet, the majority of information remains in print. A forward-looking, twenty-first century library recognizes this and cultivates an environment where print and digital media are not placed at odds, but thrive side by side. This companion reflects this ideology, bridging the gap between traditional and digital sources. Remember, it is not a question of Web or print; it is a question of finding the *best* information. Users of this companion will get the most out of it if they draw selectively from both its print and Web resources. Also, keep in mind what kind of information each medium offers. The Web sites included in this volume tend to be most useful as background materials that supplement your readings. For example, many of the sites contain helpful biographical information or provide study guides and overviews that aid in understanding specific works of literature. There are certainly good examples of secondary criticism online, and this companion makes every effort to identify them. Print materials, however, still tend to be more useful for locating secondary resources for researching paper topics. Thus, users who need help finding sources that help explain Shakespeare's sonnets may be content with the content of Web sites, whereas users writing papers on Shakespeare's sonnets may want to dig into print resources and, if available, make good use of the *MLA International Bibliography* discussed briefly subsequently.

Also keep in mind that Web sites often go down or change locations. Although many of the sites in this companion can be counted on to remain stable or, at the very least, to provide a redirect if the address changes, after time the addresses of some of the sites may no longer work. This could be especially true of the study guides, for which addresses may change as classes move from semester to semester. The best advice is this: if a link is down, don't give up. First, simply try again later; the site might be down only temporarily. If the site has not come back up, try paring back the address to the next "/." For example if the address http://faculty.goucher.edu/eng211/george_herbert.htm is down, pare down the address to http://faculty.goucher.edu/eng211/ and see if you can find a new link to the document you are looking for. If this fails, try searching Google.com using some of the key works given in the entry's annotation. If the annotation reads, "Study notes on Herbert's *The Temple*. From Prof. Sanders of Goucher College," try searching the terms "Herbert," "The Temple," and "Sanders" to see if you can find a new link or another site that connects to it. You may also be able to view a cached version of the site, an option when using Google.

Continue to Research

For optimal success, users will want to continue their research using online databases to which their library may subscribe. (If you are not sure to which literature-related databases your library subscribes, check your library's home page or talk with a reference librarian.) To find journal articles on an author or topic, the standard resources are the electronic version of the *MLA International Biography* and the *Annual Bibliography of English Language and Literature*. *MLA International Bibliography,* probably the most used database in the field of English literature, indexes more than 4,400 journals from the years 1960 to the present and should be available at most colleges and universities. Users may want to consult a reference librarian for tips on how to search these databases most efficiently.

Want to view Renaissance books as they were first published in the sixteenth and seventeenth centuries? Your institution may subscribe to *Early English Books Online,* which contains PDF (portable document format) reproductions of most of the books listed in Pantzer, Pollard, and Redgrave's *Short-Title Catalogue* (1475–1640) and Wing's *Short-Title Catalogue* (1641–1700). Your institution may also subscribe to the *English Poetry Database, English Prose Drama Database,* and *English Verse Drama.* These databases contain the full text of Renaissance works (and much more), and users may search them by words or phrases in the text.

Don't forget about print sources. For exhaustive supplements to this companion, consult James L. Harner's *Literary Research Guide: An Annotated Listing of Reference Sources in English Literary Studies* (New York: Modern Language Association of America, 2002) and Bracken's *Reference Works in British and American Literature,* cited earlier.

Finally, make full use of your library. Drop by the reference desk and talk with librarians about your project. They will be happy to help.

Frequently Cited Web Sites

Acheson, Kathy. English 1710b: Female Dramatists of the English Seventeenth Century. Course Home Page. May 1997–Aug. 1997. University of Waterloo. 8 June 2003, http://english.uwaterloo.ca/courses/engl710b/.
   Contains bibliographies of secondary sources on Elizabeth I, Mary Sidney, Elizabeth Cary, and Mary Wroth.

Archive for the History of Economic Thought. Ed. Rod Hay. Update unknown. McMaster University. 8 June 2003, http://www.socsci.mcmaster.ca/econ/ugcm/3ll3/.
   "This archive is an attempt to collect in one place a large number of significant texts in the history of economic thought." Includes entries on Renaissance thinkers such as Thomas Hobbes and James Harrington.

As One Phoenix: Four Seventeenth-Century Women Poets. Ed. Ron Cooley. 19 June 1998. University of Saskatchewan. 8 June 2003, http://www.usask.ca/english/phoenix/homepage3.htm.
   A site devoted to the seventeenth-century poets Margaret Cavendish, Aemilia Lanyer, Katherine Philips, and Lady Mary Wroth.

Best, Michael. Early Shakespeare: A Short Course. Course Home Page. 6 May 1997. University of Victoria. 23 June 2003, http://www.engl.uvic.ca/Faculty/Best/ISShakespeare/ShortCourse.html.
   Prof. Best's Web site for a course on Shakespeare's early works. Provides introductory modules for *Love's Labour's Lost, Richard II, Romeo and Juliet*, and the sonnets.

Best, Michael. English 364: Home Page. Course Home Page. Jan. 2003–Apr. 2003. University of Victoria. 23 June 2003, http://english.uvic.ca/Faculty/MBHomePage/engl364/.
   Professor Best's Web site for his class on English Renaissance drama. Provides informative pages on Elizabeth Cary's *Tragedy of Mariam*, Christopher Marlowe's *Doctor Faustus*, Thomas Dekker's *The Shoemakers' Holiday*, John Marston's *The Malcontent*, Benjamin Jonson's *Bartholomew Fair*, and Francis Beaumont's *The Knight of the Burning Pestle*.

Boyer, Norman. English 201: English Literature to 1700: Links to Reading Questions for Major Works, fall 2001. Saint Xavier University. 8 June 2003, http://english.sxu.edu/boyer/fall01/201_questlist_f01.htm.
   Study questions for Marlowe's *Doctor Faustus*, Book I of Spenser's *Faerie Queen*, John Webster's *The Duchess of Malfi*, and John Milton's *Paradise Lost*.

The Brown University Women Writers Project. Ed. Julia Flanders, Syd Bauman, and Paul Caton. Update unknown. Brown University. 8 June 2003, http://www.wwp.brown.edu/.
   A site devoted to the study of early modern women writers. Includes a wealth of electronic texts.

"The Cambridge History of English and American Literature." *Bartleby. com.* 8 June 2003, http://www.bartleby.com/216/.

Although the printed edition on which this site is based is nearly a century old, this resource maintains a detail and depth that is often difficult to find on the Internet. Still, because of its age, it is recommended that this site be used in collaboration with modern resources.

Catholic Encyclopedia. Ed. Kevin Knight. 20 Apr. 2003. 8 June 2003, http://www. newadvent.org/cathen/.

An online reproduction of the 1908 *Catholic Encyclopedia.* This resource remains one of the finest religion-related encyclopedias and is particularly helpful to this companion for it entries on religious writers of the Renaissance.

Christian Classics Ethereal Library. Ed. Harry Plantinga, et al. Update unknown. Calvin College. 8 June 2003, http://www.ccel.org/.

An online collection of "Classic Christian Books." Includes works by Richard Baxter, Jeremy Taylor, and Richard Hooker.

Early Modern Literary Studies. Ed. Lisa Hopkins. May 2003. 23 June 2003, http://www. shu.ac.uk/emls/emlshome.html.

A refereed, online journal examining "English literature, literary culture, and language during the sixteenth and seventeenth centuries." An excellent source for current secondary criticism. Also contains other useful information including reviews of electronic resources and calls for papers.

Early Tudor Texts. Ed. Laine G. M. Ruus. 1 Dec. 2001. University of Toronto, Data Library Service. 8 June 2003, http://www.chass.utoronto.ca/datalib/codebooks/ utm/tudor.htm.

Contains the full text of many early Tudor works.

Elizabethan Authors: Texts, Resources, and Authorship Sites. Ed. Robert Brazil and Barboura Flues. Update unknown. 23 June 2003, http://www.elizabethanauthors. com/.

Provides electronic texts, biographies, and bibliographies for Renaissance authors such as Thomas Kyd, Robert Greene, Thomas Nashe, and Gabriel Harvey. A good site for information on the often-overlooked authors of the period.

Emory Women Writers Resource Project. Ed. Leigh Tillman Partington. 1998. Emory University. 8 June 2003, http://chaucer.library.emory.edu/cgi-bin/sgml2html/ wwrp.pl.

A collection of electronic texts written by women writers. Sometimes includes introductory essays and biographical information.

"Encyclopaedia Britannica Presents Shakespeare and the Globe: Then and Now." Ed. and update unknown. *Encyclopaedia Britannica.* 8 June 2003, http://search.eb.com/ shakespeare/.

As informative as it is attractive, this site is a great starting place for Shakespeare online, including a set of pages devoted to Shakespeare's Globe Theatre. The biographies section contains helpful information on many of Shakespeare's contemporaries and on Shakespearean actors, both Elizabethan and modern.

Englishhistory.net. Ed. Marilee Hanson. Update unknown. 25 June 2003, http://www.
  englishhistory.net/.
  A history site with a section devoted to "Tudor England: 1485 to 1603" that includes information on Tudor monarchs, the six wives of Henry VIII, frequently asked
questions about Tudor England, a Tudor bibliography, and portraits of the Tudors and
their contemporaries.

"The English Renaissance in Context (ERIC)." Ed. Rebecca Bushnell, Michael Ryan,
  and Brett Wilson. Update unknown. University of Pennsylvania. 8 June 2003, http://
  oldsite.library.upenn.edu/etext/collections/furness/eric/teach/index.htm.
  Features several well-designed multimedia tutorials covering topics in the history
of the book and Shakespeare's *King Lear, The Merchant of Venice, Richard III,* and *Romeo and Juliet.*

Foxe Digital Project Home Page. Ed. and update unknown. The Ohio State University
  Libraries. 8 June 2003, http://dlib.lib.ohio-state.edu/ foxe/index.php.
  Contains a wealth of PDF images from the 1563, 1570, 1576, and 1583 editions of
John Foxe's *Book of Martyrs (Acts and Monuments).*

The Galileo Project. Eds. Albert Van Helden and Elizabeth Burr. Update unknown. Rice
  University. 8 June 2003, http://es.rice.edu/ES/humsoc/Galileo/Catalog/Files/
  more.html.
  "A hypertext source of information on the life and work of Galileo Galilei
(1564–1642) and the science of his time." Additionally includes biographies of his contemporaries found by searching the "Catalog of the Scientific Community of the 16th
and 17th Centuries."

Harley, David. Ideas in Society, 1500–1700. Course Home Page. Jan. 2001–May 2001.
  University of Notre Dame. 8 June 2003, http://www.nd.edu/~dharley/HistIdeas/
  coursepage.html.
  Click on the course schedule link to find links to brief biographies and bibliographies of primary and secondary works on many early modern thinkers.

"History of the Monarchy." *Official Web site of the British Monarchy.* Ed. and update
  unknown. 24 June 2003, http://www.royal.gov.uk/output/ Page5.asp.
  "Choose an English Dynasty" or link to the sections "Kings and Queens of England (to 1603)," "Kings and Queens of Scotland (to 1603)," and "Kings and Queens of
the United Kingdom (from 1603)" for detailed historical and biographical information
on British monarchs.

The Internet Encyclopedia of Philosophy. Eds. James Fieser and Bradley Dowden. Update unknown. University of Tennessee at Martin. 8 June 2003, http://www.
  utm.edu/research/iep/.
  An online Internet Encyclopedia with entries on Renaissance thinkers such as
Francis Bacon and Edward Herbert of Cherbury.

Jacobean Drama. Ed. J. M. Massi. 12 Mar. 1997. 26 June 2003, http://www.
  jetlink.net/~massij/jacob/index.shtml.
  Provides study guides for selected Jacobean plays. Particularly helpful for its
guides on non-Shakespearean drama, including Francis Beaumont's *The Knight of the
Burning Pestle, The Revenger's Tragedy,* John Webster's *The Duchess of Malfi,* and
John Ford's *Tis Pity She's a Whore.*

Johnston, Ian. English 366: Studies in Shakespeare, Spring 2001. Course Home Page. 28 Dec. 2003. Malaspina University-College. 25 Jun 2003, http://www.mala.bc.ca/ ~johnstoi/eng366/lectures/lectures.htm.

Scroll down for links to comprehensive introductory lectures for Shakespeare's *Antony and Cleopatra, As You Like It, Hamlet, Henry IV Part One, Henry V, King Lear, Macbeth, Richard II, Richard III, The Tempest,* and *Twelfth Night.*

Kinney, Clare. English 381: The History of Literature in English I. Course Home Page. 6 Sep. 1999. The University of Virginia. 8 June 2003, http://faculty.virginia. edu/engl381ck/.

Click on the link for "Lecture Highlights" for study notes on various Renaissance authors. Also features a lovely art gallery.

Luminarium. Ed. Anniina Jokinen. 7 Apr. 2003. 8 June 2003, http://www. luminarium.org/lumina.htm.

A gem of a Web site and an excellent starting place for students in the field of Renaissance literature. In addition to her own primary resources, such as biographies and full text transcriptions of texts, Jokinen clearly has made an effort to bring together the best sites related to medieval and Renaissance English writers.

Mooney, Jennifer. English 3024: Renaissance Literature. Course Home Page. Jan. 2003–May 2003. Virginia Polytechnic Institute and State University. 23 June 2003, http://athena.english.vt.edu/~jmooney/ renhome.htm.

The home page for Professor Mooney's Renaissance literature course. Contains a wealth of study guides ranging from Thomas More to John Milton. The links to the study guides are found on the "Calendar" page.

The Norton Anthology of English Literature: Norton Topics Online. Ed. Eileen Connell, et al. Update unknown. W. W. Norton and Company. 8 June 2003, http://www. wwnorton.com/nael/.

An online companion to the *Norton Anthology of English Literature* containing four supplemental topics for each of the literary time periods covered. Current topics of the sixteenth century are the following: "The Magician, the Heretic, and the Playwright" (related to Marlowe's *Faustus*), "Renaissance, Exploration, Travel, and the World outside Europe," "Dissent, Doubt, and Spiritual Violence in the Reformation," and "Island Nations." Current topics for the early seventeenth century are the following: "Gender, Family, Households," "*Paradise Lost* in Context," "Civil Wars of Ideas" and "Emigrants and Settlers." Each topic contains the sections "texts and contexts," "explorations," "Web resources," and "illustrations."

The Penn State Archive of Samuel Johnson's Lives of the Poets. Ed. Kathleen Nulton Kemmerer. 28 Mar. 2001. Penn State University. 8 June 2003, http://www. hn.psu.edu/faculty/kkemmerer/poets/main.htm.

Samuel Johnson's *Lives of the Poets* transcribed from *Prefaces, Biographical and Critical, to The Works of the English Poets.*

Poetry Archive. Ed. and update unknown. 8 June 2003, http://www.poetry-archive. com/.

An extensive online collection of poetry.

Poets Corner. Eds. Bob Blair, Jon Lachelt, Nelson Miller, and Steve Spanoudis. Update
   unknown. 8 June 2003, http://www.theotherpages.org/poems/.
   An exhaustive collection of online poetry that features the work of more than 780
poets.

Poets.org. Ed. Melissa Ozawa. 21 May 2003. The Academy of American Poets. 8 June
   2003, http://www.Poets.org/.
   The Web site for the Academy of American Poets. This site is helpful for finding
information on poets of the English Renaissance. Use "Find a Poet" to search for entries
that include a portrait of the poet (when available), a biography, and links to full text selections of their poetry.

Project Gutenberg. Ed. Michael Hart. 4 May 2003. 9 June 2003, http://gutenberg.net/.
   An online publisher and repository of more than six thousand electronic texts. A
great place to find books online.

Renascence Editions. Ed. Richard Bear. 12 June 2003, http://darkwing.uoregon.edu/
   ~rbear/ren.htm.
   Providing electronic texts of English works written between 1477 and 1799, this is
one of the best sites for full text editions of Renaissance works. Created and maintained
by Richard Bear of the University of Oregon.

Representative Poetry Online. Ed. Ian Lancashire. 19 Dec. 2002. University of Toronto
   Libraries. 8 June 2003, http://eir.library.utoronto.ca/rpo/display/index.cfm.
   Transcribes 2,500 poems of 203 British and American poets from the Old English
period to the present. Includes notes on the publication history and bio-bibliographic information. The material can be accessed by author, title, first line, publication date of poems, or by keyword search. The site also lists a general bibliography, a glossary of
poetry terms and forms, and a timeline of poets, poems, and events.

Sanders, Arnie. English 211: English Literature, Beowulf to Dryden. Course Home
   Page. 26 May 2003. Goucher College. 23 June 2003, http://faculty.goucher.edu/
   eng211/.
   Helpful study notes for many English Renaissance writers including Philip Sidney,
Edmund Spenser, William Shakespeare, Ben Jonson, and John Milton.

Scanned Texts. Ed. Jack Lynch. Update unknown. Rutgers University, Newark. 8 June
   2003, http://www.andromeda.rutgers.edu/~jlynch/Texts/.
   Full text editions of late-seventeenth-, eighteenth-, and nineteenth- century British
texts. Scanned and edited by Jack Lynch of Rutgers University, Newark.

Scottish Authors. Ed. unknown. 23 Apr. 2001. Scottish Library Association. 8 June
   2003, http://www.slainte.org.uk/scotauth/scauhome.htm.
   The online version of the Scottish Library Association's *Discovering Scottish
Writers*. Contains concise biographies of Scottish writers from all time periods. Authors
are listed both alphabetically and chronologically.

Shakespeare's Life and Times. Ed. Michael Best. 3 July 2003. University of Victoria. 8
   June 2003, http://web.uvic.ca/shakespeare/Library/SLT/.
   A comprehensive Shakespeare site. Features ten "books" devoted to Shakespearean topics, including "Shakespeare's life," "the stage," "the drama," and "some plays
explored." A great resource for online Shakespearean research. Also provides valuable
introductions to the culture of Renaissance England.

Smith, Jon. English 245, Survey III: Renaissance and Restoration. Course Home Page. Jan. 2003–Apr. 2003. Hanover College. 8 June 2003, http://smith.hanover. edu/eng245sq.html.

   A Web site supplementing Smith's Renaissance and Restoration course. Click on "Study Questions" for links to pages covering Renaissance authors including John Skelton, Isabella Whitney, Edmund Spenser, Sir Philip Sidney, Christopher Marlowe, William Shakespeare, John Donne, and John Milton.

Sonnet Central. Ed. Eric Blomquist. 29 Jan. 2002. Sonnets.org. 8 June 2003, http:// www.sonnets.org/.

   "An archive of English sonnets, commentary, and relevant web links and a forum for poets to share and discuss their own work." Useful for its wealth of sonnets written by the likes of Surrey, Wyatt, Spenser, Shakespeare, and Donne.

Stanford Encyclopedia of Philosophy. Ed. Edward N. Zalta. Stanford University. 8 June 2003, http://plato.stanford.edu/.

   An excellent online resource for students of philosophy.

Theatre Study Packets. Ed. and update unknown. Brigham Young University, Theatre and Media Arts Department. 8 June 2003, http://www.nauvoo.byu.edu/TheArts/ Theater/studypackets/main.cfm.

   Study guides produced by the Brigham Young University Theatre Department to supplement their productions. Includes Dekker's *The Shoemaker's Holiday* and Shakespeare's *Comedy of Errors, Henry V, Julius Caesar, Macbeth, The Merry Wives of Windsor, A Midsummer Night's Dream,* and *Romeo and Juliet.*

Theatrehistory.com. Ed. and update unknown. 8 June 2003, http://www.theatrehistory. com/.

   Helpful for finding biographies of Renaissance playwrights. Keep in mind, however, that the texts are normally taken from early-twentieth-century encyclopedias and other public domain works. Therefore, be sure to use this resource in collaboration with up-to-date sources.

Willbern, David. "Early Shakespeare": English 309. Course Home Page. Jan 2001–Apr. 2001. The University of Buffalo. 24 June 2003, http://www.cas.buffalo.edu/ classes/eng/willbern/Shakespeare/plays/index309. htm.

   Includes separate Web sites for each of the plays covered in the course: *As You Like It, The Comedy of Errors, Henry IV Part One, Julius Caesar, The Merchant of Venice, A Midsummer Night's Dream, Richard III, Richard II, Romeo and Juliet,* and *Titus Andronicus.* Each site features study questions, lecture notes, and links to related sites.

———. "Later Shakespeare": English 310. Course Home Page. Aug. 2002–Sep. 2002. The University of Buffalo. 24 June 2003, http://www.cas.buffalo.edu/ classes/eng/willbern/Shakespeare/index310. htm.

   Includes separate Web sites for each of the plays covered in the course: *Antony and Cleopatra, Hamlet, King Lear, Macbeth, Measure for Measure, Othello, The Tempest,* and *Twelfth Night.* Each site features study questions, lecture notes, and links to related sites.

Zauhar, Frances Murphy. EL 315: Shakespeare's Comedies and Tragedies. Course Home Page. Jan. 2001–May 2001. Saint Vincent College. 8 June 2003, http://facweb.stvincent.edu/Academics/English/el315/ 315lectures.html.

   Features slideshow lectures on Shakespeare's *Hamlet, The Merchant of Venice, A Midsummer Night's Dream,* and *The Taming of the Shrew.*

Frequently Cited References

Baker, William, and Kenneth Womack. *Pre-Nineteenth-Century British Book Collectors and Bibliographers* (Dictionary of Literary Biography 213). Detroit: Gale, 1999.

Battestin, Martin C., ed. *British Novelists, 1660–1800* (Dictionary of Literary Biography 39). Detroit: Gale, 1985.

Bowers, Fredson. *Elizabethan Dramatists* (Dictionary of Literary Biography 62). Detroit: Gale, 1987.

———. *Jacobean and Caroline Dramatists* (Dictionary of Literary Biography 58). Detroit: Gale, 1987.

Bracken, James K., and Joel Silver. *British Literary Booktrade, 1475–1700* (Dictionary of Literary Biography 170). Detroit: Gale, 1996.

Dematteis, Philip B., and Peter S. Fosl, *British Philosophers, 1500–1799* (Dictionary of Literary Biography 252). Detroit: Gale, 2002.

Hager, Alan, ed. *Major Tudor Authors: A Bio-Bibliographical Critical Sourcebook.* Westport, Conn.: Greenwood, 1997.

Hester, M. Thomas. *Seventeenth-Century British Nondramatic Poets: First Series* (Dictionary of Literary Biography 121). Detroit: Gale, 1992.

———. *Seventeenth-Century British Nondramatic Poets: Second Series* (Dictionary of Literary Biography 126). Detroit: Gale, 1993.

———. *Seventeenth-Century British Nondramatic Poets: Third Series* (Dictionary of Literary Biography 131). Detroit: Gale, 1993.

Lein, Clayton D. *British Prose Writers of the Early Seventeenth Century* (Dictionary of Literary Biography 151). Detroit: Gale, 1995.

Dennis Poupard, et al., eds. *Literature Criticism from 1400 to 1800.* Detroit: Gale, 1984–.

Malone, Edward A. *British Rhetoricians and Logicians, 1500–1660: First Series* (Dictionary of Literary Biography 236). Detroit: Gale, 2000.

Richardson, David A. *Sixteenth-Century British Nondramatic Writers. First Series* (Dictionary of Literary Biography 132). Detroit: Gale, 1993.

Richardson, David A. *Sixteenth-Century British Nondramatic Writers. Second Series* (Dictionary of Literary Biography 136). Detroit: Gale, 1994.

Richardson, David A. *Sixteenth-Century British Nondramatic Writers. Third Series* (Dictionary of Literary Biography 167). Detroit: Gale, 1996.

Richardson, David A. *Sixteenth-Century British Nondramatic Writers. Fourth Series* (Dictionary of Literary Biography 172). Detroit: Gale, 1996.

Walker, Kim. *Women Writers of the English Renaissance.* New York: Twayne, 1996.

Web Sites and References for English Renaissance Authors

Lancelot Andrewes, 1555–1626

Web Sites

Hutchinson, F. E. "Andrewes and Donne Compared." *Bartleby.com.* 7 June 2003, http://www.bartleby.com/214/1211.html.
    An essay on Andrewes and John Donne from *The Cambridge History of English and American Literature,* 1907–1921.

"Lancelot Andrewes (1555–1626)." *Luminarium.* 7 June 2003, http://www.luminarium.org/sevenlit/andrewes/.
    A comprehensive Web site on Andrewes.

"Lancelot Andrewes 1555–1626." *Library of Anglo-Catholic Theology: Project Canterbury.* Ed. Richard Mammana. Update unknown. Society of Archbishop Justus. 8 June 2003, http://justus.anglican.org/resources/pc/lact/.
    Links to the full text of Andrewes's sermons.

Biographies and Criticism

"Lancelot Andrewes." *Literature Criticism from 1400 to 1800* 5: 17–43.
    Excerpts of comments and criticism on Andrewes from 1631–1984.

Owen, Trevor A. "Lancelot Andrewes." Lein, *British Prose Writers of the Early Seventeenth Century* (Dictionary of Literary Biography 151), 9–20.

Shuger, Debora K. "Lancelot Andrewes." Richardson, *Sixteenth-Century British Nondramatic Writers,* 4th ser. (Dictionary of Literary Biography 172), 3–9.

Roger Ascham, 1515/16–1568

Web Sites

"The Life of Ascham by Samuel Johnson." *Electronic Texts.* 8 June 2003, http://andromeda.rutgers.edu/~jlynch/Texts/ascham.html.
    The text of Samuel Johnson's biography of Ascham edited by Jack Lynch of Rutgers University.

"Roger Ascham (1515–1568)." *Luminarium.* 8 June 2003, http://www.luminarium.org/renlit/ascham.htm.
    A comprehensive Web site on Ascham.

"The Scholemaster (1570)." *Renascence Editions*. 8 June 2003, http://darkwing. uoregon.edu/%7Erbear/ascham1.htm.
>The full text of Ascham's *The Scholemaster*.

Woodward, W. H. "Roger Ascham." *Bartleby.com*. 8 June 2003, http://www.bartleby. com/213/1911.html.
>The entry on Ascham from "English Universities, Schools, and Scholarship in the Sixteenth Century," in *The Cambridge History of English and American Literature*, 1907–1921.

Biographies and Criticism

Nelson, Brent L. "Roger Ascham." Malone, *British Rhetoricians and Logicians, 1500–1660,* 1st ser. (Dictionary of Literary Biography 236), 3–11.

Ryan, Lawrence V. *Roger Ascham*. Stanford: Stanford UP, 1963.

Bibliographies

Dees, Jerome Steele. *Sir Thomas Elyot and Roger Ascham: A Reference Guide*. Boston: G. K. Hall, 1981.

Anne Askew, 1521–1546

Web Sites

"Anne Askew." *Spartacus Educational*. Ed. and update unknown. 8 June 2003, http://www.spartacus.schoolnet.co.uk/TUDaskew.htm.
>Includes of brief biography, a detail of the woodcut illustration of Askew's execution from John Foxe's *Book of Martyrs (Acts and Monuments)* (1563), and brief excerpts from *The Examinations of Anne Askew* and *Book of Martyrs*.

"Dissent, Doubt, and Spiritual Violence in the Reformation: Texts and Contexts." *The Norton Anthology of English Literature: Norton Topics Online*. 8 June 2003, http://www.wwnorton.com/nael/16century/ topic_3/askwexam.htm.
>Contains excerpts from John Foxe's *Book of Martyrs* and *The First Examination of Anne Askew*. Also provides many helpful materials concerning the English Reformation, including an overview, "explorations" linked to Reformation texts, and links to online resources.

Foxe Digital Project Home Page. The Ohio State University Libraries. 8 June 2003, http://dlib.lib.ohio-state.edu/foxe/index.php.
>Contains PDF images of the martyrdom of Anne Askew from the 1563, 1570, 1576, and 1583 editions of John Foxe's *Book of Martyrs*.

"Selected Poetry of Anne Askew (1521–1546)." *Representative Poetry Online*. 8 June 2003, http://eir.library.utoronto.ca/rpo/display/poet428. html.
>The full text of "The Ballad which Anne Askew made and sang when she was in Newgate," with a brief note on Askew's life and works.

Biographies and Criticism

"Anne Askew." *Literature Criticism from 1400 to 1800* 81: 88–144.
Excerpts of comments and criticism on Askew from 1981–1998.

Beilin, Elaine V. "Anne Askew." Richardson, *Sixteenth-Century British Nondramatic Writers,* 2d ser. (Dictionary of Literary Biography 136), 7–11.

Bibliographies

Hansard-Weiner, Sonja. "Anne Askew." Hager, *Major Tudor Authors,* 20–24.
Brief biography, survey of major works and themes, critical reception, and bibliography of works by and about Askew.

Francis Bacon, 1561–1626

Web Sites

"*Essays* (1625) by Sir Francis Bacon (1561–1626)." *UTEL (University of Toronto English Library).* Eds. Dennis G. Jerz and Christopher Douglas. Update unknown. University of Toronto English Library. 8 June 2003, http://www.library. utoronto.ca/utel/criticism/baconf_ess/ess_titlepage.html.
Contains the full text of Bacon's *Essays* (1625).

"Francis Bacon.*" Internet Archive of Texts and Documents.* 8 June 2003, http://history. hanover.edu/texts/bacon/bactable.html.
The full text of *The Great Instauration* with links to other works by Bacon. Created and maintained by the History Department of Hanover College

"Sir Francis Bacon (1561–1626)." *Luminarium.* 8 June 2003, http://www. luminarium.org/sevenlit/bacon/.
A comprehensive Web site on Bacon.

Sorely, W. R. "The Beginnings of English Philosophy: Francis Bacon." *Bartleby.com.* 8 June 2003, http://www.bartleby.com/214/#14.
Entries on Bacon from *The Cambridge History of English and American Literature,* 1907–21. Includes a biography and essays on his philosophical works.

Biographies and Criticism

Briggs, John Channing. "Francis Bacon." Lein, *British Prose Writers of the Early Seventeenth Century* (Dictionary of Literary Biography 151), 21–39.

Davies, Rosalind. "Francis Bacon." Dematteis and Fosl, *British Philosophers, 1500–1799* (Dictionary of Literary Biography 252), 11–36.

Green, Adwin Wigfall. *Sir Francis Bacon.* New York: Twayne, 1966.

Skerpan-Wheeler, Elizabeth. "Francis Bacon." Malone, *British Rhetoricians and Logicians, 1500–1660,* 1st ser. (Dictionary of Literary Biography 236), 12–39.

"Sir Francis Bacon." *Literature Criticism from 1400 to 1800* 18: 98–198.
    Excerpts of comments and criticism on Bacon from 1605–1988.

"Sir Francis Bacon." *Literature Criticism from 1400 to 1800* 32: 104–190.
    Excerpts of comments and criticism on Bacon from 1627–1993.

Sessions, William A. *Francis Bacon Revisited.* New York: Twayne, 1996.

Indexes and Concordances

Davies, David William, and Elizabeth S. Wrigley. *A Concordance to the Essays of Francis Bacon.* Detroit: Gale, 1973.
    Based on the text of J. Spedding, R. L. Ellis, and D. D. Heath's edition of *The Works of Francis Bacon* (London: Longman, 1857–1874).

Bibliographies

Asher, Lyell. "Francis Bacon." Hager, *Major Tudor Authors,* 25–29.
    Brief biography, survey of major works and themes, critical reception, and bibliography of works by and about Bacon.

John Bale, 1495–1563

Web Sites

Berkhout, Carl T. "Bale, John." *Anglo-Saxonists—16th Century.* Update unknown. University of Arizona. 8 June 2003, http://www.u.arizona.edu/~ctb/16abcd.html#jbale.
    A brief Bale bibliography compiled by Carl Berkhout from the University of Arizona.

"Biography of John Bale." *The 1911 Edition Encyclopedia.* 8 June 2003, http://93.1911encyclopedia.org/B/BA/BALE_JOHN.htm.
    A biography of Bale reproduced from an unnamed "1911 encyclopedia."

Early Tudor Texts. 8 June 2003, http://www.chass.utoronto.ca/datalib/codebooks/utm/tudor.htm.
    Contains the full text of Bale's *King Johan, A Tragedy or enterlude manyfestyng the chefe promyses of God* and *A brefe Comedy or enterlude concernynge the temptacyon of our lorde and sauer Jesus Christ by Sathan in the desart.* Note: the latter two texts are written in ASCII-tagged texts and are somewhat difficult to read.

Biographies and Criticism

Bale, John. *The Vocacyon of Johan Bale.* Eds. Peter Happé and John N. King. Binghamton, N.Y.: Medieval and Renaissance Texts and Studies in conjunction with Renaissance English Text Society, 1990.

Happé, Peter. *John Bale.* New York: Twayne, 1996.

"John Bale." *Literature Criticism from 1400 to 1800* 62: 1–67.
    Excerpts of comments and criticism on Bale from 1838–1996.

King, John N. "Jc in Bale." Richardson, *Sixteenth-Century British Nondramatic Writers,* 1st ser. *(*Dictio ary of Literary Biography 132), 27–35.

Alexander Barclay, 1475?–1552

Web Sites

Koelbing, Arthur. "Barclay and Skelton." *Bartleby.com.* 9 June 2003, http://www. bartleby.com/213/index.html#4.
Essays on Barclay's life and works from *The Cambridge History of English and American Literature,* 1907–1921.

Biographies and Criticism

Carlson, David R. "Alexander Barclay." Richardson, *Sixteenth-Century British Nondramatic Writers,* 1st ser. (Dictionary of Literary Biography 132), 36–47.

Richard Barnfield, 1574–1627

Web Sites

"Barnfield, Richard (1574–1620?)." *GLBTQ: An Encyclopedia of Gay, Lesbian, Bisexual, Transgender, & Queer Culture.* Ed. George Klawitter. 4 Feb. 2002. 8 June 2003, http://www.glbtq.com/literature/barnfield_r.html.
A detailed look at the life and career of Barnfield with attention given to his homoerotic verse.

Lee, Sidney. "Richard Barnfield." *Bartleby.com.* 8 June 2003, http://www.bartleby.com/213/1213.html.
A brief biography of Barnfield from *The Cambridge History of English and American Literature,* 1907–21.

"Richard Barnfield 1574–1620." Ed. George Klawitter. Update unknown. St. Edward's University. 8 June 2003, http://www.stedwards.edu/hum/klawitter/barnfield/barnfield.html.
An illustrated site dedicated to the life of Barnfield from Professor Klawitter at St. Edward's University.

"Selected Poetry of Richard Barnfield (1574–1627)." *Representative Poetry Online.* 8 June 2003, http://eir.library.utoronto.ca/rpo/display/ poet13.html.
Features the full text of Barnfield's "An Ode" and "To His Friend Master R. L., In Praise of Music and Poetry."

Biographies and Criticism

Borris, Kenneth. "Richard Barnfield." Richardson, *Sixteenth-Century British Nondramatic Writers,* 4th ser. (Dictionary of Literary Biography 172), 10–26.

Borris, Kenneth, and George Klawitter, Eds. *The Affectionate Shepherd: Celebrating Richard Barnfield.* Selinsgrove, Penn.: Susquehanna UP; London: Associated University Presses, 2001.

Richard Baxter, 1615–1691

Web Sites

Christian Classics Ethereal Library. 8 June 2003, http://www. ccel.org/index/author-B.html.
Scroll down to the entry for Baxter for links to the full text of his *Reformed Pastor* and *Saints' Everlasting Rest.*

Hutton, W. H. "Caroline Divines." *Bartleby.com.* 8 June 2003, http://www.bartleby. com/217/#6.
Three essays on Baxter: "Richard Baxter," "*The Saints' Everlasting Rest,*" and "The sermons at Paul's Cross." From *The Cambridge History of English and American Literature,* 1907–21.

The Richard Baxter Homepage. Ed. Dale Tedder. 25 May 2001. 9 June 2003, http:// members.aol.com/augusteen/Baxter.html.
Provides a comprehensive collection of links to Baxter resources online, including biographies and online editions of his works.

The Richard Baxter Society. Ed. unknown. 15 Feb. 1998. Richard Baxter Society. 14 June 2003, http://members.tripod.com/~oboofcom/index-3. html.
Features a brief biography and links to Baxter resources online. Keep an eye out for the future construction of an online library of articles from the Society's journal *Baxter Notes & Studies.*

Biographies and Criticism

Keeble, N. H. *Richard Baxter, Puritan Man of Letters.* Oxford: Clarendon P; New York: Oxford UP, 1982.

Francis Beaumont, 1584–1616

Web Sites

"Beaumont and Fletcher: List of Plays and Poems." *Drama and Poems of Beaumont and Fletcher.* Ed. Paul Ellison. Update unknown. University of Exeter. 8 June 2003, http://www.ex.ac.uk/~pellison/BF/playlist.htm.
A complete list of the works written by Beaumont and Fletcher, both collaboratively and individually. Includes the full texts of some works, including *The Knight of the Burning Pestle* and *The Maid's Tragedy.*

"Beaumont, Francis." *Encyclopaedia Britannica Presents Shakespeare and the Globe: Then and Now.* 8 June 2003, http://www.britannica.com/shakespeare/micro/58/ 62.html.
A concise biography of Beaumont. Includes bibliographies of his major works and of selected biographies and criticism.

"Francis Beaumont (1584–1616)." *Luminarium.* 8 June 2003, http://www.luminarium. org/sevenlit/beaumont/.
A comprehensive Web site on Beaumont.

"Francis Beaumont: A Biographical Sketch." *Theatrehistory.com.* 8 June 2003, http://www.theatrehistory.com/british/beaumont001.html.
> A biography of Beaumont originally published in William Allan Neilson's *Chief Elizabethan Dramatists* (New York: Houghton Mifflin Company, 1911).

"Francis Beaumont, *The Knight of the Burning Pestle*." Ed. Timothy Billings. Update unknown. Middlebury College. 8 June 2003, http://f00.middlebury.edu/LI101C/beaumont.html.
> Study notes on Beaumont's play from Professor Billings of Middlebury College.

Macaulay, G. C. "Beaumont and Fletcher." *Bartleby.com.* 8 June 2003, http://www.bartleby.com/216/#5.
> The entry on Beaumont and Fletcher from *The Cambridge History of English and American Literature,* 1907–21. Includes biographical essays, as well as discussions of their work.

"*Philaster or Love Lies Bleeding*: A Synopsis of the Play by Beaumont & Fletcher." *TheatreHistory.com.* 8 June 2003, http://www.theatrehistory.com/british/beaumont002.html.
> A synopsis of *Philaster* originally published in Fort and Kates's *Minute History of the Drama* (New York: Grosset & Dunlap, 1935).

Biographies and Criticism

Bliss, Lee. *Francis Beaumont.* Boston: Twayne, 1987.

"Francis Beaumont and John Fletcher." *Drama Criticism* 6: 39–116.
> Excerpts of criticism on Beaumont and Fletcher in general and on *Philaster, The Maid's Tragedy,* and *A King and No King* from 1940–1989, with an annotated bibliography.

"Francis Beaumont and John Fletcher." *Literature Criticism from 1400 to 1800* 33: 38–100.
> Excerpts of comments and criticism on Beaumont and Fletcher from 1901–1990.

Hoy, Cyrus. "Francis Beaumont and John Fletcher." Bowers, *Jacobean and Caroline Dramatists* (Dictionary of Literary Biography 58), 3–26.

Bibliographies

Collier, Susanne. "Francis Beaumont." Hager, *Major Tudor Authors,* 29–32.
> Brief biography, survey of major works and themes, critical reception, and bibliography of works by and about Beaumont.

Robert Boyle, 1627–1691

Web Sites

MacIntosh J. J. "Robert Boyle." *Stanford Encyclopedia of Philosophy.* 8 June 2003, http://plato.stanford.edu/entries/boyle/.
> A comprehensive biography of Boyle with a bibliography and selected Boyle related links.

The Robert Boyle Project. Ed. Michael Hunter. Update unknown. University of London.
8 June 2003, http://www.bbk.ac.uk/Boyle/.
"The Official Robert Boyle Website." Features a biographical introduction to Boyle,
a bibliography, and recent news in Boyle studies.

Biographies and Criticism

Hunter, Michael, ed. *Robert Boyle Reconsidered.* Cambridge and New York: Cambridge UP, 1994.

Bibliographies

Fulton, John F. *A Bibliography of the Honourable Robert Boyle, Fellow of the Royal Society.* Oxford: Clarendon P, 1961.

Nicholas Breton, 1555?–1626

Web Sites

Poets Corner. 8 June 2003, http://www.theotherpages.org/poems/poem-ab.html#breton.
A selection of Breton's poems, including "Phillida and Coridon," "Who Can Live
in Heart So Glad," and "An Odd Conceit."

"Selected Poetry of Nicholas Breton (1555?–1626)." *Representative Poetry Online.* 8
June 2003, http://eir.library.utoronto.ca/rpo/display/poet28.html.
The full text of "The Passionate Shepherd."

Biographies and Criticism

Nielson, James. "Nicholas Breton." Richardson, *Sixteenth-Century British Nondramatic
Writers,* 2d. ser. (Dictionary of Literary Biography 136), 28–37.

Richard Brome, c. 1590–1652/3

Web Sites

"Brome, Richard." *Encyclopaedia Britannica Presents Shakespeare and the Globe:
Then and Now.* 8 June 2003, http://www.britannica.com/shakespeare/micro/87/
68.html.
A concise biography of Brome.

"Richard Brome—A Selective Bibliography." Ed. Matthew Steggle. Update unknown.
Sheffield Hallam University. 8 June 2003, http://www.shu.ac.uk/schools/cs/
teaching/ms/projects/brome/brome.htm.
A selected bibliography of works by and about Brome.

Biographies and Criticism

Clark, Ira. *Professional Playwrights: Massinger, Ford, Shirley, & Brome.* Lexington,
Ky.: UP of Kentucky, 1992.

Nania, John S. "Richard Brome." Bowers, *Jacobean and Caroline Dramatists* (Dictionary of Literary Biography 58), 26–36.

"Richard Brome." *Literature Criticism from 1400 to 1800* 61: 128–222.
Excerpts of comments and criticism on Brome from 1912–1992.

Sanders, Julie. *Caroline Drama: The Plays of Massinger, Ford, Shirley, and Brome.* Plymouth: Northcote House, in association with the British Council, 1999.

Shaw, Catherine M. *Richard Brome.* Boston: Twayne, 1980.

Sir Thomas Browne, 1605–1682

Web Sites

Johnson, Samuel. "The Life of Browne." *Electronic Texts.* 8 June 2003, http://andromeda.rutgers.edu/~jlynch/Texts/browne.html.
The text of Samuel Johnson's biography of Browne edited by Jack Lynch of Rutgers University.

Saintsbury, George. "Antiquaries." *Bartleby.com.* 8 June 2003, http://www.bartleby.com/217/index.html#10.
Essays on the life and works of Browne from *The Cambridge History of English and American Literature,* 1907–21.

"Sir Thomas Browne." Ed. James Eason. Update unknown. University of Chicago. 14 June 2003, http://penelope.uchicago.edu/.
Features the full text of Browne's major works, including facsimiles in PDF format. Also has Johnson's *Life of Browne.* Created by James Eason at the University of Chicago.

"Sir Thomas Browne (1605–1682)." *Luminarium.* 8 June 2003, http://www.luminarium.org/sevenlit/browne/.
A comprehensive Web site on Browne.

Westfall, Richard S. "Browne, Thomas." *The Galileo Project.* 8 June 2003, http://es.rice.edu/ES/humsoc/Galileo/Catalog/Files/browne.html.
A detailed outline of Browne's life by Professor Westfall of Indiana University.

Biographies and Criticism

Huntley, Frank Livingstone. *Sir Thomas Browne, a Biographical and Critical Study.* Ann Arbor: U Michigan P, 1962.

Post, Jonathan F. S. *Sir Thomas Browne.* Boston: Twayne, 1987.

Seelig, Sharon Cadman. "Sir Thomas Browne." Lein, *British Prose Writers of the Early Seventeenth Century* (Dictionary of Literary Biography 151), 55–68.

Bibliographies

Donovan, Dennis G. *Sir Thomas Browne 1924–1966; Robert Burton 1924–1966.* London: Nether P, 1968.

Donovan, Dennis G, Magaretha G. Hartley Herman, and Ann E. Imbrie. *Sir Thomas Browne and Robert Burton: A Reference Guide.* Boston: G. K. Hall, 1981.

William Browne of Tavistock, 1590?–1645?

Web Sites

De Sélincourt, Hugh. "The Successors of Spenser: William Browne." *Bartleby.com.* 8 June 2003, http://www.bartleby.com/214/0903.html.
　　An entry on Browne's literary career from *The Cambridge History of English and American Literature,* 1907–21.

"Selected Poetry of William Browne (1590?–1645)." *Representative Poetry Online.* 8 June 2003, http://eir.library.utoronto.ca/rpo/display/poet35.html.
　　An excerpt from Browne's *Britannia's Pastorals.*

Biographies and Criticism

Riddell, James A. "William Browne of Tavistock." Hester, *Seventeenth- Century British Nondramatic Poets,* 1st ser. (Dictionary of Literary Biography 121), 36–44.

John Bunyan, 1628–1688

Web Sites

Bronte, Judith. "A Timeline Chronicling the Life of John Bunyan." Update Unknown. 8 June 2003, http://acacia.pair.com/Acacia.John.Bunyan/John.Bunyan.Timeline.html.
　　A detailed timeline of the life of Bunyan. Explore the site for other features including the full text of many of Bunyan's works.

Brown, John. "John Bunyan. Andrew Marvell." *Bartleby.com.* 8 June 2003, http://www.bartleby.com/217/#7.
　　Essays on the life and work of Bunyan from *The Cambridge History of English and American Literature,* 1907–21.

"The International John Bunyan Society." Ed. David Gay. Update unknown. University of Alberta. 8 June 2003, http://www.arts.ualberta.ca/~dgay/Bunyan.htm.
　　Provides information on the society, the *Bunyan Studies* journal, and conference announcements.

John Bunyan Online. Ed. and update unknown. Mount Zion Online. 8 June 2003, http://www.johnbunyan.org/.
　　"The largest online archive of everything Bunyan." Contains the works of Bunyan in HTML, RTF, TXT, and PDF formats.

"*The Pilgrim's Progress.*" *Renascence Editions.* 8 June 2003, http://www.uoregon.edu/~rbear/bunyan1.html.
　　The full text of Bunyan's *Pilgrim's Progress.*

Biographies and Criticism

Damrosch, Leopold, Jr. "John Bunyan." Battestin, *British Novelists, 1660–1800* (Dictionary of Literary Biography 39), 1: 79–89.

"John Bunyan." *Literature Criticism from 1400 to 1800* 4: 140–207.
    Excerpts of comments and criticism on Bunyan from 1767–1984.

"John Bunyan." *Literature Criticism from 1400 to 1800* 69: 1–112.
    Excerpts of comments and criticism on Bunyan from 1985–2000.

Sadler, Lynn Veach. *John Bunyan.* Boston: Twayne, 1979.

Bibliographies

Batson, E. Beatrice. *John Bunyan's Grace Abounding and the Pilgrim's Progress: An Overview of Literary Studies, 1960–1987.* New York: Garland, 1988.

Forrest, James F., and Richard Lee Greaves. *John Bunyan: A Reference Guide.* Boston: G. K. Hall, 1982.

Wharey, James Blanton. *The Pilgrim's Progress From This World to That Which is to Come.* Oxford: Clarendon P, 1960.

Robert Burton, 1577–1640

Web Sites

"*The Anatomy of Melancholy* by Robert Burton." *Complete Review.* Ed. and update unknown. 8 June 2003, http://www.complete-review.com/reviews/divphil/burtonr.htm.
    A review of Burton's *The Anatomy of Melancholy* with quotes from the text. Could be used as a helpful overview of the text.

Bensly, Edward. "Robert Burton, John Barclay and John Owen." *Bartleby.com.* 8 June 2003, http://www.bartleby.com/214/#13.
    Essays on Burton from *The Cambridge History of English and American Literature,* 1907–21. Includes a biography and essays on his *The Anatomy of Melancholy.*

Biographies and Criticism

Dixon, Barbara Hart. "Robert Burton." Lein, *British Prose Writers of the Early Seventeenth Century* (Dictionary of Literary Biography 151), 69–76.

O'Connell, Michael. *Robert Burton.* Boston: Twayne, 1986.

"Robert Burton." *Literature Criticism from 1400 to 1800* 74: 97–247.
    Excerpts of comments and criticism on Burton from 1776–1998.

Bibliographies

Conn, Joey. *Robert Burton and the Anatomy of Melancholy: An Annotated Bibliography of Primary and Secondary Sources*. New York: Greenwood, 1988.

Donovan, Dennis G. *Sir Thomas Browne 1924–1966; Robert Burton 1924–1966*. London: Nether P, 1968.

Donovan, Dennis G, Magaretha G. Hartley Herman, and Ann E. Imbrie. *Sir Thomas Browne and Robert Burton: A Reference Guide*. Boston: G. K. Hall, 1981.

Samuel Butler, 1613–1680

Web Sites

"The Iliad." *The Internet Classics Archive*. Ed. Daniel C. Stevenson. 4 Oct. 2000. Massachusetts Institute of Technology. 8 June 2003, http://classics.mit.edu/Homer/iliad.html.
The full text of Butler's translation of Homer's *Iliad*.

Johnson, Samuel. "The Life of Samuel Butler." *The Penn State Archive of Samuel Johnson's Lives of the Poets*. 8 June 2003, http://www.hn.psu.edu/Faculty/KKemmerer/poets/butler/default.html.
The full text of Johnson's life of Butler.

"Samuel Butler." *Project Gutenberg*. 9 June 2003, http://digital.library.upenn.edu/webbin/gutbook/author?name=Butler%2C%20Samuel.
Features the full text of Butler's works, including *Hudibras*.

"Selected Poetry of Samuel Butler (1613–1680)." *Representative Poetry Online*. 8 June 2003, http://eir.library.utoronto.ca/rpo/display/poet43.html.
An excerpt from part one of Butler's *Hudibras*.

Smith, William Francis. "Samuel Butler." *Bartleby.com*. 8 June 2003, http://www.bartleby.com/218/#2.
The entry on Butler from *The Cambridge History of English and American Literature,* 1907–21. Includes essays on his life and works.

Biographies and Criticism

Holt, Lee E. *Samuel Butler*. Boston: Twayne, 1989.

Horne, William C. "Samuel Butler." Siebert, *British Prose Writers, 1660–1800,* 1st ser. (Dictionary of Literary Biography 101), 77–87.

"Samuel Butler." *Literature Criticism from 1400 to 1800* 16: 1–57.
Excerpts of comments and criticism on Butler from 1693–1989.

"Samuel Butler." *Literature Criticism from 1400 to 1800* 43: 59–135.
Excerpts of comments and criticism on Butler from 1925–1996.

Troost, Linda V. "Samuel Butler." Hester, *Seventeenth-Century British Nondramatic Poets,* 2d. ser. (Dictionary of Literary Biography 126), 27–41.

Wasserman, George Russell. *Samuel "Hudibras" Butler*. Boston: Twayne, 1989.

Bibliographies

Wasserman, George Russell. *Samuel Butler and the Earl of Rochester: A Reference Guide*. Boston: G. K. Hall, 1986.

William Camden, 1551–1623

Web Sites

"*Annales Rerum Gestarum Angliae et Hiberniae Regnante Elizabetha (1615 and 1625) with the annotations of Sir Francis Bacon*." Ed. Dana Sutton. 1 Feb. 2001. University of California, Irvine. 8 June 2003, http://eee.uci.edu/~papyri/camden/.
The full text of Camden's work in Latin and English.

Whibley, Charles. "William Camden." *Bartleby.com*. 8 June 2003, http://www. bartleby.com/213/1506.html.
The entry on Camden from *The Cambridge History of English and American Literature*, 1907–1921.

"William Camden (1551–1563)." *Luminarium*. 8 June 2003, http://www.luminarium. org/encyclopedia/camden.htm.
Contains a biography of Camden with links to other Camden-related Internet sites and a brief bibliography of secondary resources.

"William Camden." *Anthropology Biography Web*. Update unknown. Minnesota State University, Mankato. 8 June 2003, http://emuseum. mnsu.edu/information/biography/ abcde/camden_william.html.
Provides a short biography of Camden. Created by anthropology students at Minnesota State University, Mankato.

Biographies and Criticism

Herendeen, Wyman H. "William Camden." Richardson, *Sixteenth-Century British Nondramatic Writers*, 4th ser. (Dictionary of Literary Biography 172), 25–37.

Thomas Campion, 1567–1620

Web Sites

Bayne, Ronald. "Campion's Masques." *Bartleby.com*. 8 June 2003, http://www. bartleby.com/216/1308.html.
An entry on Campion's masques from *The Cambridge History of English and American Literature*, 1907–21.

"The Latin Poetry of Thomas Campion (1567–1620) a hypertext edition." Ed. Dana F. Sutton. 23 May 1999. University of California, Irvine. 8 June 2003, http://eee. uci.edu/~papyri/campion/.
An electronic edition of Campion's Latin poetry in Latin and in translation. Edited by Professor Dana F. Sutton of the University of California, Irvine.

"Selected Poetry of Thomas Campion (1567–1620)." *Representative Poetry Online*. 8 June 2003, http://eir.library.utoronto.ca/rpo/display/poet50.html.
The full text of a selection of Campion's poems.

"Thomas Campion." *Poets.org*. 8 June 2003, http://www.poets.org/poets/poets.cfm?prmID=300.
A biography of Campion from the Academy of American Poets.

"Thomas Campion (1567–1620)." *Luminarium*. 8 June 2003, http://www.luminarium.org/renlit/campion.htm.
A comprehensive Web site on Campion.

Vivian, S. Percival. "Thomas Campion." *Bartleby.com*. 9 June 2003, http://www.bartleby.com/214/#8.
Entries on Campion from *The Cambridge History of English and American Literature,* 1907–1921. Includes a biography and essays on "His Work" and "His Prosody."

Biographies and Criticism

Davis, Walter R. *Thomas Campion*. Boston: Twayne, 1987.

Lindley, David. "Thomas Campion." Bowers, *Jacobean and Caroline Dramatists* (Dictionary of Literary Biography 58), 37–44.

"Thomas Campion." *Literature Criticism from 1400 to 1800* 78: 1–94.
Excerpts of comments and criticism on Campion from 1913–1987.

Thomas Carew, 1594/5–1640

Web Sites

"The Cavalier Poets." 8 June 2003, http://athena.english.vt.edu/~jmooney/renmats/cavaliers.htm.
Brief study notes on Carew and the cavalier poets.

Moorman, F. W. "Cavalier Lyrists: Thomas Carew." *Bartleby.com*. 8 June 2003, http://www.bartleby.com/217/0109.html.
An essay on the life and works of Carew from *The Cambridge History of English and American Literature,* 1907–21.

Pursglove, Glyn. "Carew, Thomas." *Literary Encyclopedia and Literary Dictionary*. Eds. Robert Clark, Emory Elliott, and Janet Todd. 20 Oct. 2002. Literaryencyclopedia.com. 8 June 2003, http://www. literaryencyclopedia.com/cgi-bin/eautname.pl?author1=CarewXXThomas.
A biography of Carew.

"Selected Poetry of Thomas Carew (1595?–1640)." *Representative Poetry Online*. 8 June 2003, http://eir.library.utoronto.ca/rpo/display/ poet53.html.
A selection of Carew's poems, including "An Elegy upon the Death of the Dean of St. Paul's, Dr. John Donne," "A Song: When June is past, the fading rose," and "To My Inconstant Mistress."

"Thomas Carew (1594–1640)." *Luminarium*. 8 June 2003, http://www.luminarium. org/sevenlit/carew/.
A comprehensive Web site on Carew.

Biographies and Criticism

Parker, Michael P. "Thomas Carew." Hester, *Seventeenth-Century British Nondramatic Poets,* 2d ser. (Dictionary of Literary Biography 126), 42–54.

Sadler, Lynn Veach. *Thomas Carew*. Boston: Twayne, 1979.

"Thomas Carew." *Literature Criticism from 1400 to 1800* 13: 1–69.
Excerpts of comments and criticism on Carew from 1632–1988.

"Thomas Carew." *Poetry Criticism* 29: 1–90.
Excerpts of comments and criticism on Carew from 1964–1989, with an annotated bibliography.

Lady Elizabeth Cary, 1585–1639

Web Sites

"Elizabeth Cary: Bibliography." *Female Dramatists of the English Seventeenth Century.* 8 June 2003, http://english.uwaterloo.ca/courses/ engl710b/carybib.html.
Contains a bibliography of secondary sources on Cary.

Hamlin, William. "Elizabeth Cary's *Mariam* and the Critique of Pure Reason." *Early Modern Literary Studies* 9, no .1 (May 2003): 2.1–22. 8 June 2003, http:// purl.oclc.org/emls/09-1/hamlcary.html.
An article on Cary's *The Tragedy of Mariam.*

"The Tragedy of Mariam." 8 June 2003, http://www.engl.uvic.ca/Faculty/ MBHomePage/engl364/mariamtoc.html.
A Web site devoted to Cary's *The Tragedy of Mariam.* Includes background materials on Senecan rhetoric and "the role of the sexes." Also provides an excerpt from Elizabeth Cary's diary and a bibliography of further reading that includes print and online resources.

Biographies and Criticism

"Elizabeth Tanfield Cary, Viscountess Falkland." *Literature Criticism From 1400 to 1800* 30: 156–178.
Excerpts of comments and criticism on Cary from 1985–1991.

Walker, Kim. " 'By publike language grac't': Elizabeth Cary, Lady Falkland." *Women Writers of the English Renaissance.* New York: Twayne, 1996, 124–145.

Bibliographies

Cavanagh, Sheila T. "Elizabeth Cary." Hager, *Major Tudor Authors*, 59–64.
Brief biography, survey of major works and themes, critical reception, and bibliography of works by and about Cary.

Douglas, Krystan V. "Cary, Elizabeth." *Guide to British Drama Explication*, 49. New York: G. K. Hall, 1996.

Morra, Irene. "Elizabeth Cary." Ed. Mary R. Reichardt. *Catholic Women Writers,* 24–28. Westport, Conn.: Greenwood, 2001.
Brief biography and survey of themes and criticism, with lists of selected works by and about Cary.

Margaret Lucas Cavendish, Duchess of Newcastle, 1623–1723

Web Sites

"Atomic Poems of Margaret (Lucas) Cavendish, Duchess of Newcastle." *Emory Women Writers Resource Project*. 8 June 2003, http://chaucer.library.emory.edu/cgi-bin/ sgml2html/wwrp.pl.
Scroll down to "Cavendish" to link to the "Atomic Poems" from her 1653 edition of *Poems and Fancies*. Features modern introductory essays to the text and biographical information.

Fitzmaurice, James. "Margaret Cavendish Bibliography." *British Literature: Modern and Early Modern*. Update unknown. Northern Arizona University. 8 June 2003, http://jan.ucc.nau.edu/~jbf/CavBiblio.html.
Maintained by a Cavendish scholar, this excellent site lists recent and forthcoming publications, and various editions of her works.

"Margaret Cavendish, Duchess of Newcastle." *As One Phoenix: Four Seventeenth-Century Women Poets*. 8 June 2003, http://www.usask.ca/english/phoenix/cavendishm.htm.
Biography, bibliography, and a list of poems from *Poems and Fancies* (1653).

"Margaret Cavendish, Duchess of Newcastle (1631–1673)." *Ideas in Society, 1500–1700*. 8 June 2003, http://www.nd.edu/~dharley/HistIdeas/ MargCavendish. html.
A brief biography and a selected bibliography of primary and secondary works. Includes many links to online texts.

The Margaret Cavendish Society. Ed. Nancy Weitz. Update unknown. Oxford University. 8 June 2003, http://users.ox.ac.uk/~nancy/marcav/.
An unadorned and simple-to-navigate site where users can access the society's newsletters and publication abstracts from past Cavendish conferences (1998–). There is also a decent list of electronic resources: articles, Cavendish texts, historically relevant sites, and links to women writers and literary period sites.

"Margaret (Lucas) Cavendish, Duchess of Newcastle (1623–1673)." *Luminarium*. 8 June 2003, http://www.luminarium.org/sevenlit/cavendish/.
A comprehensive Web site on Cavendish.

"Margaret Lucas Cavendish (1623–74)." *Great Voyages: The History of Western Philosophy*. Ed. Bill Uzgalis. Jan. 1999. Oregon State University. 8 June 2003, http://oregonstate.edu/instruct/phl302/philosophers/ cavendish.html.
A detailed timeline of Cavendish's life.

Biographies and Criticism

Bonin, Erin Lang. "Margaret Cavendish, Duchess of Newcastle." Dematteis and Fosl, *British Philosophers, 1500–1799* (Dictionary of Literary Biography 252), 107–115.

"Margaret Cavendish." *Literature Criticism from 1400 to 1800* 30: 179–236.
Excerpts of comments and criticism on Cavendish from 1925–1992.

Miller, Steven Max. "Margaret Lucas Cavendish, Duchess of Newcastle." Hester, *Seventeenth-Century British Nondramatic Poets,* 3d ser. (Dictionary of Literary Biography 131), 36–48.

Bibliographies

"Margaret Cavendish, Duchess of Newcastle." *New Cambridge Bibliography of English Literature* 1:1303, 1736, 2252.

William Caxton, c. 1422–1491

Web Sites

Duff, E. Gordon. "The Introduction of Printing into England and the Early Work of the Press: William Caxton." *Bartleby.com.* 8 June 2003, http://www.bartleby.com/212/1302.html.
The entry on Caxton from *The Cambridge History of English and American Literature,* 1907–1921.

"Printing in England from William Caxton to Christopher Barker, An Exhibition: November 1976 - April 1977." *Glasgow University Library Special Collections.* Ed. Julie Gardham. 5 May 2003. Glasgow University. 8 June 2003, http://special.lib.gla.ac.uk/exhibns/printing/.
An illustrated look at Caxton's career. A part of a larger exhibit on early English printing.

Shedden, Neil. "William Caxton." *Renaissance Reflections.* Update unknown. 8 June 2003, http://home.vicnet.net.au/~neils/renaissance/caxton.htm.
Provides a brief biography of Caxton and a few links to sites concerning early printing.

Warren, K. M. "William Caxton." *Catholic Encyclopedia.* 8 June 2003, http://www.newadvent.org/cathen/03469a.htm.
A concise biography of Caxton reproduced from the 1908 *Catholic Encyclopedia.*

"William Caxton Preface to *Morte Darthur*." *The Norton Anthology of English Literature: Norton Topics Online.* 8 June 2003, http://www. wwnorton.com/nael/middleages/topic_2/caxton.htm.
A supplement to *The Norton Anthology of English Literature* providing a brief biography of Caxton and the full text of his preface to *Morte Darthur.*

Biographies and Criticism

Blake, N. F. *Caxton: England's First Publisher*. London: Osprey, 1976.

Penninger, Frieda Elaine. *William Caxton*. Boston: Twayne, 1979.

Vann, J. Donn. "William Caxton." Bracken and Silver, *British Literary Booktrade, 1475–1700* (Dictionary of Literary Biography 170), 48–58.

"William Caxton." *Literature Criticism from 1400 to 1800* 17: 1–41.
    Excerpts of comments and criticism on Caxton from 1877–1987.

Bibliographies

Blake, N. F. *William Caxton: A Bibliographical Guide*. New York: Garland, 1985.

Kindrick, Robert L., and Ruth E. Hamilton. "William Caxton." Hager, *Major Tudor Authors*, 73–77.
    A brief biography, survey of major works and themes, critical reception, and bibliography of works by and about Caxton.

George Chapman, 1559?–1634

Web Sites

"Chapman, George." *Encyclopaedia Britannica Presents Shakespeare and the Globe: Then and Now*. 8 June 2003, http://www.britannica.com/shakespeare/micro/116/80.html.
    A concise biography of Chapman. Includes bibliographies of his major works and of selected biographies and criticism.

"George Chapman." *Theatrehistory.com*. 8 June 2003 http://www.theatrehistory.com/british/chapman001.html.
    A concise biography of Chapman taken from the *Encyclopedia Britannica*, 1910.

"The Odysseys of Homer, translated according to the Greek by George Chapman." *Bartleby.com*. 8 June 2003, http://www.bartleby.com/111/.
    The full text of Chapman's translation of Homer's *Odyssey*. Reproduced from an 1857 edition (London: J.R. Smith).

"Selected Poetry of George Chapman (1559?–1634)." *Representative Poetry Online*. 8 June 2003, http://eir.library.utoronto.ca/rpo/display/ poet59.html.
    Contains the full text of "A Coronet for his Mistress, Philosophy" and excerpts from Chapman's translation of Homer's *Odyssey* and *Iliad*.

Biographies and Criticism

Braden, Gordon. "George Chapman." Bowers, *Elizabethan Dramatists* (Dictionary of Literary Biography 62), 3–29.

"George Chapman." *Literature Criticism from 1400 to 1800* 22: 1–85.
    Excerpts of comments and criticism on Chapman from 1681–1985.

Snare, Gerald. "George Chapman." Hester, *Seventeenth-Century British Nondramatic Poets,* 1st ser. (Dictionary of Literary Biography 121), 45–58.

Bibliographies

Beach, Vincent W. *George Chapman: An Annotated Bibliography of Commentary and Criticism.* New York: G. K. Hall; London: Prentice Hall, 1995.

Huntington, John W. "George Chapman." Hager, *Major Tudor Authors,* 78–83.
    A brief biography, survey of major works and themes, critical reception, and bibliography of works by and about Chapman.

Pennel, Charles A., and William P. Williams. *George Chapman. John Marston.* London: Nether P, 1968.

Charles I, 1600–1649

Web Sites

"Charles I (r. 1625–49)." *Kings and Queens of England to 1603.* 8 June 2003, http://www.royal.gov.uk/output/Page76.asp.
    A detailed biography of Charles I from the official Web site of the British Monarchy.

Biographies and Criticism

"Charles I." *Literature Criticism from 1400 to 1800* 13: 138–155.
    Excerpts of comments and criticism on Charles I from 1649–1987.

John Cleveland, 1613–1658

Web Sites

"Selected Poetry of John Cleveland (1613–1658)." *Representative Poetry Online.* 8 June 2003, http://eir.library.utoronto.ca/rpo/display/poet67. html.
    The full text of Cleveland's "On the Memory of Mr. Edward King, Drown'd in the Irish Seas."

Biographies and Criticism

Jacobus, Lee A. *John Cleveland.* New York: Twayne, 1975.

Jaeckle, Daniel P. "John Cleveland." Hester, *Seventeenth-Century British Nondramatic Poets,* 2d ser. (Dictionary of Literary Biography 126), 62–70.

Bibliographies

Morris, Brian Robert. *John Cleveland (1613–1658): A Bibliography of His Poems.* London: Bibliographical Society, 1967.

Richard Corbett, 1582–1635

Biographies and Criticism

"Richard Corbett (1582–1635): Bishop and Poet." *The Corbett Study Group.* Ed. J. C.
Noble. 15 May 2003. The Corbett Study Group. 8 June 2003, http://website.
lineone.net/~corbett_group3/Fourth/bishop.htm.
A biography of Corbett.

Web Sites

Papazian, Mary Arshagouni. "Richard Corbett." Hester, *Seventeenth-Century British
Nondramatic Poets,* 1st ser. (Dictionary of Literary Biography 121), 59–67. –1921

Abraham Cowley, 1618–1667

Web Sites

"Abraham Cowley (1618–1667)." *Luminarium.* 8 June 2003, http://www.luminarium.
org/sevenlit/cowley/.
A comprehensive Web site on Cowley.

"Selected Poetry of Abraham Cowley (1618–1667)." *Representative Poetry Online.* 9
June 2003, http://eir.library.utoronto.ca/rpo/display/poet78.html.
The full text of selected poems of Cowley including "The Given Heart," "On the
Death of Mr. Crashaw," and excerpts from *Anacreon* and *Davideis.*

Spingarn, J. E. "Jacobean and Caroline Criticism: D'Avenant and Cowley." *Bartleby.
com.* 8 June 2003, http://www.bartleby.com/217/1108.html.
A brief essay on Cowley's criticism from *The Cambridge History of English and
American Literature,* 1907–1921.

Sprat, Thomas. "An Account of the Life and Writings of Mr. Abraham Cowley (1668)."
Representative Poetry Online. 8 June 2003, http://eir.library.utoronto.ca/rpo/
display/displayprose.cfm?prosenum=10.
The full text of Sprat's introduction to *The Works of Mr. Abraham Cowley,* 1668.

Thompson, A. Hamilton. "Writers of the Couplet." *Bartleby.com.* 8 June 2003,
http://bartelby.com/217/index.html#3.
Five essays on Cowley's poetic works from *The Cambridge History of English and
American Literature,* 1907–1921.

Biographies and Criticism

"Abraham Cowley." *Literature Criticism from 1400 to 1800* 43: 136–199.
Excerpts of comments and criticism on Cowley from 1779–1977.

Anselment, Raymond. "Abraham Cowley." Lein, *British Prose Writers of the Early Seventeenth Century* (Dictionary of Literary Biography 151), 105–113.

Calhoun, Thomas O. "Abraham Cowley." Hester, *Seventeenth-Century British Nondramatic Poets,* 3d ser. (Dictionary of Literary Biography 131), 61–72.

Taaffe, James G. *Abraham Cowley.* New York: Twayne, 1972.

Bibliographies

Perkin, M. R. *Abraham Cowley: A Bibliography.* Folkestone, England: Dawson, 1977.

Richard Crashaw, 1612/13–1649

Web Sites

Hutchinson, F. E. "The Sacred Poets." *Bartleby.com.* 8 June 2003, http://www. bartleby.com/217/index.html#2.
　　Five essays on Crashaw from *The Cambridge History of English and American Literature,* 1907–1921.

"Richard Crashaw." *Catholic Encyclopedia.* 8 June 2003, http://www.newadvent.org/ cathen/04467a.htm.
　　A detailed biography of Crashaw reproduced from the 1908 *Catholic Encyclopedia.*

"Richard Crashaw (1613–1649)." *Luminarium.* 8 June 2003, http://www.luminarium. org/sevenlit/crashaw/.
　　A comprehensive Web site on Crashaw.

"Richard Crashaw, *Steps to the Temple, The Delights of the Muses* (1646) and *Carmen Deo Nostro* (1652)." 9 June 2003, http://faculty.goucher.edu/eng211/richard _crashaw.htm.
　　Study notes on Crashaw.

"Selected Poetry of Richard Crashaw (1613–1649)." *Representative Poetry Online.* 9 June 2003, http://eir.library.utoronto.ca/rpo/display/poet84.html.
　　A selection of Crashaw's poems including "In the Holy Nativity of Our Lord" and an excerpt from "The Flaming Heart."

Biographies and Criticism

Cousins, A. D. *The Catholic Religious Poets from Southwell to Crashaw: A Critical History.* London: Sheed & Ward, 1991.

Healy, Thomas F. *Richard Crashaw.* Leiden: E. J. Brill, 1986.

Parrish, Paul A. *Richard Crashaw.* Boston: Twayne, 1980.

"Richard Crashaw." *Literature Criticism from 1400 to 1800* 24: 1–79.
　　Excerpts of comments and criticism on Crashaw from 1652–1991.

Sabine, Maureen. "Richard Crashaw." Hester, *Seventeenth-Century British Nondramatic Poets,* 2d ser. (Dictionary of Literary Biography 126), 71–86.

Indexes and Concordances

Cooper, Robert M., and Sundaram Swetharanyam. *A Concordance to the English Poetry of Richard Crashaw*. Troy, N.Y.: Whitson, 1980.

Bibliographies

Roberts, John Richard. *Richard Crashaw: An Annotated Bibliography of Criticism, 1632–1980*. Columbia: U Missouri P, 1985.

Samuel Daniel, 1562?–1619

Web Sites

Child, Harold H. "Robert Southwell. Samuel Daniel." *Bartleby.com*. 8 June 2003, http://www.bartleby.com/214/#7.
　　A brief biography of Daniel and an essay on his *Delia, The Complaynt of Rosamond, and Musophilus*. From *The Cambridge History of English and American Literature*, 1907–21.

Renascence Editions. Eds. Richard Bear and Thomas Larque. 8 June 2003, http://darkwing.uoregon.edu/~rbear/ren.htm#d.
　　Features the full text of *A Defence of Rhyme* and *Delia. Contayning certayne Sonnets: with the complaint of Rosamond*.

"Samuel Daniel (1562–1619)." *Luminarium*. 8 June 2003, http://www.luminarium.org/renlit/daniel.htm.
　　A comprehensive Web site on Daniel.

"Selected Poetry of Samuel Daniel (1562–1619)." *Representative Poetry Online*. 8 June 2003, http://eir.library.utoronto.ca/rpo/display/poet87.html.
　　Includes the full text of selections from *Delia,* and excerpts from *Musophilus* and *The Civil Wars*.

Biographies and Criticism

Harner, James L. "Samuel Daniel." Bowers, *Elizabethan Dramatists* (Dictionary of Literary Biography 62), 30–39.

"Samuel Daniel." *Literature Criticism from 1400 to 1800* 24: 80–146.
　　Excerpts of comments and criticism on Daniel from 1662–1989.

Seronsy, Cecil. *Samuel Daniel*. New York: Twayne, 1967.

Bibliographies

Guffey, George Robert. *Samuel Daniel, 1942–1965. Michael Drayton, 1941–1965. Sir Philip Sidney, 1941–1965*. London: Nether P, 1967.

Harner, James L. *Samuel Daniel and Michael Drayton: A Reference Guide*. Boston: G. K. Hall, 1980.

Klein, Lisa Mary. "Samuel Daniel." Hager, *Major Tudor Authors,* 105–109.
  A brief biography, survey of major works and themes, critical reception, and bibliography of works by and about Daniel.

William D'Avenant, 1606–1668

Web Sites

"Davenant, Sir William." *Encyclopaedia Britannica Presents Shakespeare and the Globe: Then and Now.* 8 June 2003, http://www.britannica.com/shakespeare/micro/160/59.html.
  A concise biography of D'Avenant.

"Selected Poetry of Sir William D'Avenant (1606–1668)." *Representative Poetry Online.* 8 June 2003, http://eir.library.utoronto.ca/rpo/display/poet88.html.
  The full text of the "Preface" to *Gondibert, an Heroick Poem.*

"Sir William D'Avenant." *Catholic Encyclopedia.* 8 June 2003, http://www.newadvent.org/cathen/04639b.htm.
  A concise biography of D'Avenant reproduced from the 1908 *Catholic Encyclopedia.*

"*The Tempest; or, The Enchanted Island* by William Davenant and John Dryden." *Electronic Texts.* 8 June 2003, http://newark.rutgers.edu/~jlynch/Texts/tempest.html.
  The full text of D'Avenant and Dryden's play.

Thompson, A. Hamilton. "Writers of the Couplet. Sir William D'Avenant; Gondibert." *Bartleby.com.* 9 June 2003, http://www.bartleby.com/217/0312.html.
  An essay on D'Avenant and his epic poem *Gondibert* from *The Cambridge History of English and American Literature,* 1907–1921.

Biographies and Criticism

Bordinat, Philip. *Sir William Davenant.* Boston: Twayne, 1981.

Cauthen, Irby B. "Sir William Davenant." Bowers, *Jacobean and Caroline Dramatists* (Dictionary of Literary Biography 58), 59–72.

Durant, Jack D. "Sir William Davenant." Hester, *Seventeenth-Century British Nondramatic Poets,* 2d ser. (Dictionary of Literary Biography 126), 87–96.

"William Davenant." *Literature Criticism from 1400 to 1800* 13: 156–220.
  Excerpts of comments and criticism on D'Avenant from 1640–1984.

Bibliographies

Blaydes, Sophia B., and Philip Bordinat. *Sir William Davenant: An Annotated Bibliography, 1629–1985.* New York: Garland, 1986.

John Davies, 1569–1626

Web Sites

Sélincourt, Hugh De. "Sir John Davies." *Bartleby.com.* 8 June 2003, http://www.bartleby.com/214/0905.html.
The entry on Davies from *The Cambridge History of English and American Literature,* 1907–1921.

"Sir John Davies (1569–1626)." *Luminarium.* 8 June 2003, http://www.luminarium.org/renlit/davies.htm.
A comprehensive Web site on Davies.

Biographies and Criticism

Brooks, Helen B. "John Davies of Hereford." Hester, *Seventeenth-Century British Nondramatic Poets,* 1st ser.(Dictionary of Literary Biography 121), 67–77.

Sanderson, James L. *Sir John Davies.* Boston: Twayne, 1975.

Bibliographies

Klemp, P. J. *Fulke Greville and Sir John Davies: A Reference Guide.* Boston: G. K. Hall, 1985.

Thomas Dekker, 1572?–1632

Web Sites

"Dekker, Thomas." *Encyclopaedia Britannica Presents Shakespeare and the Globe: Then and Now.* 8 June 2003, http://www.britannica.com/shakespeare/micro/163/78.html.
A concise biography of Dekker.

"Dekker and Middleton, *The Roaring Girl:* Study Questions." 8 June 2003, http://smith.hanover.edu/sqroargirl.html.
Study questions for Dekker and Thomas Middleton's play *The Roaring Girl.*

"Thomas Dekker (1570? – 1632)." *Luminarium.* 8 June 2003, http://www.luminarium.org/sevenlit/dekker/.
A comprehensive Web site on Dekker.

"Thomas Dekker." *TheatreHistory.com.* 8 June 2003, http://www.theatrehistory.com/british/dekker001.html.
Reprints the Thomas Dekker biography originally published in the 1910 *Encyclopedia Britannica.*

"Thomas Dekker's *The Shoemaker's Holiday.*" Ed. Nola Smith and Bob Nelson. 8 June 2003, http://www.nauvoo.byu.edu/TheArts/Theater/studypackets/Lesson16/main.htm.
Provides biographical information and a chronology of the life of Dekker, information on the historical and theatrical backgrounds of his play *The Shoemaker's Holiday,* and an overview of its characters and structure.

Biographies and Criticism

Hoy, Cyrus. "Thomas Dekker." Bowers, *Elizabethan Dramatists* (Dictionary of Literary Biography 62), 45–70.

McLuskie, Kathleen. *Dekker and Heywood: Professional Dramatists.* New York: St. Martin's P, 1993.

Price, George R. *Thomas Dekker.* New York: Twayne, 1969.

"Thomas Dekker." *Drama Criticism* 12: 1–119.
Excerpts of criticism on Dekker in general and on *The Shoemaker's Holiday, The Honest Whore,* and *The Roaring Girl* from 1955–1997, with an annotated bibliography.

"Thomas Dekker." *Literature Criticism from 1400 to 1800* 22: 86–139.
Excerpts of comments and criticism on Dekker from 1800–1987.

Waage, Frederick O. "Thomas Dekker." Richardson, *Sixteenth-Century British Nondramatic Writers,* 4th ser. (Dictionary of Literary Biography 172), 62–71.

Indexes and Concordances

Small, V. A, P. Corballis, and J. M. Harding. *A Concordance to the Dramatic Works of Thomas Dekker.* Salzburg: Institut für Anglistik und Amerikanistik, Universität Salzburg, 1984.
Based on texts included in Fredson Bowers's standard four-volume edition, *The Dramatic Works of Thomas Dekker.*

Bibliographies

Adler, Doris Ray. *Thomas Dekker: A Reference Guide.* Boston: G. K. Hall, 1983.

Allison, Antony Francis. *Thomas Dekker, c. 1572–1632: A Bibliographical Catalogue of the Early Editions (to the end of the 17th century).* Folkestone, England: Dawsons, 1972.

Donovan, Dennis G. *Thomas Dekker, 1945–1965; Thomas Heywood, 1938–1965; Cyril Tourneur, 1945–1965.* London: Nether P, 1967.

Wolf, Janet. "Thomas Dekker." Hager, *Major Tudor Authors,* 111–117.
Brief biography, survey of major works and themes, critical reception, and bibliography of works by and about Dekker.

Thomas Deloney, 1560?–1600

Web Sites

Atkins, J. W. H. "Elizabethan Prose Fiction." *Bartleby.com.* 8 June 2003, http://www.bartleby.com/213/index.html#16.
Entries on Thomas Deloney from *The Cambridge History of English and American Literature,* 1907–1921. Includes a brief biography and essays on his *Thomas of Reading* and *Jack of Newbury.*

"Thomas Deloney's Works." *Sixteenth Century Ballads: A work in progress...*, Ed. Greg Lindahl. Update unknown. 8 June 2003, http://www.pbm.com/~lindahl/deloney/.
Scanned portions of F. O. Mann's *The Works of Thomas Deloney: Edited from the Earliest Extand Editions & Broadsides* from 1912. Contains the full text of ballads written by Deloney, along with Mann's introductory essays on Deloney and his works.

Biographies and Criticism

Halasz, Alexandra. "Thomas Deloney." Richardson, *Sixteenth-Century British Nondramatic Writers*, 3rd ser. (Dictionary of Literary Biography 167), 41–47.

"Thomas Deloney." *Literature Criticism from 1400 to 1800* 41: 71–136.
Excerpts of comments and criticism on Deloney from 1912–1995.

Wright, Eugene Patrick. *Thomas Deloney*. Boston: Twayne, 1981.

Bibliographies

Ladd, Roger A. "Thomas Deloney." Hager, *Major Tudor Authors*, 117–120.
Brief biography, survey of major works and themes, critical reception, and bibliography of works by and about Deloney.

John Denham, 1615–1669

Web Sites

"Cooper's Hill." *Electronic Texts*. 8 June 2003, http://newark.rutgers.edu/~jlynch/Texts/cooper.html.
The full text of Denham's *Cooper's Hill*. Prepared by Professor Lynch of Rutgers University.

Johnson, Samuel. "The Life of John Denham." *The Penn State Archive of Samuel Johnson's Lives of the Poets*. 8 June 2003, http://www2.hn.psu.edu/Faculty/KKemmerer/poets/denham/default.htm.
The full text of Johnson's "The Life of John Denham."

Thompson, A. Hamilton. "Writers of the Couplet: Sir John Denham." *Bartleby.com*. 8 June 2003, http://www.bartleby.com/217/0305.html.
A brief essay on Denham from *The Cambridge History of English and American Literature*, 1907–1921.

Biographies and Criticism

Champion, Larry S. "Sir John Denham." Bowers, *Jacobean and Caroline Dramatists* (Dictionary of Literary Biography 58), 80–85.

"John Denham." *Literature Criticism from 1400 to 1800* 73: 1–117.
Excerpts of comments and criticism on Denham from 1959–1998.

Skerpan, Elizabeth. "Sir John Denham." Hester, *Seventeenth-Century British Nondramatic Poets,* 2d ser. (Dictionary of Literary Biography 126), 97–108.

John Donne, 1572–1631

Web Sites

Grierson, Herbert J. C. "John Donne." *Bartleby.com.* 8 June 2003, http://www.
bartleby.com/214/index.html#11.
   The entry on Donne from *The Cambridge History of English and American Literature,* 1907–1921. Includes many biographical and critical essays.

"John Donne." *Poets.org.* 8 June 2003, http://www.poets.org/poets/poets.cfm?
prmID=247.
   A biography of Donne from the Academy of American Poets. Also includes the full text of the poems: "Air and Angels," "At the round earth's imagin'd corners," "The Bait," "Break of Day," "Death, be not proud (Holy Sonnet 10)," and "A Valediction: Forbidding Mourning."

"John Donne (1572–1631)." Ed. Kim Van Zee. 3 May 1999. Western Kentucky University. 8 June 2003, http://www2.wku.edu/~vanzekm/bio.htm.
   A site devoted to Donne containing essays on the topics "Marriage to Ann More," "Religious Conflicts," "Sonnets and Poems," and "Analysis of Several Sonnets."

"John Donne (1572–1631)." Ed. Linda Appleton. Update unknown. Abilene Christian University. 8 June 2003, http://faculty.acu.edu/~appletonl/mb1/donne.htm.
   A timeline of the "major dates and events in the life of John Donne."

"John Donne (1572–1631)." *Luminarium.* 8 June 2003, http://www.luminarium.org/
sevenlit/donne/.
   A comprehensive Web site on Donne.

"John Donne (& his Followers)." 8 June 2003, http://athena.english.vt.edu/~jmooney/
renmats/donne.htm.
   Study notes on Donne and the Metaphysical Poets.

"John Donne Journal: Studies in the Age of Donne." Ed. unknown. 31 Mar. 2000. 8 June 2003, http://social.chass.ncsu.edu/jdj/.
   The home page for the *John Donne Journal.* Contains the journal's tables of contents from 1982–1997.

"The John Donne Society Home Page." Ed. Mary Papazian. Update unknown. Oakland University. 8 June 2003, http://www2.Oakland.edu/English/donne/.
   Home to the John Donne Society. Features information on the society and its annual conference, as well as information on other Donne-related conferences.

"John Donne: Study Questions." 8 June 2003, http://smith.hanover.edu/sqdonne.html.
   Study prompts for Donne's "The Good Morrow," "Song (Go and catch a falling star)," "The Canonization," "A Valediction: Of Weeping," "The Flea," "Valediction: Forbidding Mourning," and selected Holy Sonnets. Keyed to the *Longman Anthology of British Literature,* 2nd ed.

"Selected Poetry of John Donne (1572–1631)." *Representative Poetry Online.* 8 June 2003, http://eir.library.utoronto.ca/rpo/display/poet98.html.
   A generous selection of Donne's poetry including: "The Ecstasy," "The Bait," "A Nocturnal upon St. Lucy's Day," and a selection of his Elegies, Satires, and Holy Sonnets.

"Study Guides on Donne's Poems." Ed. Theresa M. DiPasquale. Update unknown. Whitman College. 8 June 2003, http://people.whitman.edu/~dipasqtm/donne1s02. htm; http://people.whitman.edu/~dipasqtm/donne2s01.htm; http://people.whitman.edu/ ~dipasqtm/donne3s01.htm; http://people.whitman.edu/~dipasqtm/ donne4s01.htm; http://people.whitman.edu/ ~dipasqtm/donne4s02.htm.
   Links to study guides for Donne's "The Good Morrow," "The Sun Rising," "A Valediction: Forbidding Mourning," "Break of Day," "Satire 3," and the Holy Sonnets.

Biographies and Criticism

"John Donne." *Literature Criticism from 1400 to 1800* 10: 1–112.
   Excerpts of comments and criticism on Donne from 1610–1988.

"John Donne." *Literature Criticism from 1400 to 1800* 24: 147–210.
   Excerpts of comments and criticism on Donne from 1965–1993.

"John Donne." *Poetry Criticism* 1: 120–162.
   Excerpts of comments and criticism on Donne from 1618–1987, with an annotated bibliography.

Lein, Clayton D. "John Donne." Lein, *British Prose Writers of the Early Seventeenth Century* (Dictionary of Literary Biography 151), 114–139.

Parfitt, George A. E. *John Donne: A Literary Life.* Basingstoke: Macmillan, 1989.

Smith, A. J. "John Donne." Hester, *Seventeenth-Century British Nondramatic Poets,* 1st ser. (Dictionary of Literary Biography 121), 77–96.

Warnke, Frank J. *John Donne.* Boston: Twayne, 1987.

Dictionaries, Encyclopedias, and Handbooks

Ray, Robert H. *A John Donne Companion.* New York: Garland, 1990.

Indexes and Concordances

Combs, Homer Carroll, and Zay Rusk Sullens. *A Concordance to the English Poems of John Donne.* New York: Haskell House, 1969.
   Based on H. J. C. Grierson's *The Poetical Works of John Donne* (London: Oxford University Press, 1929).

Reeves, Troy Dale. *An Annotated Index to the Sermons of John Donne.* Salzburg: Institut für Anglistik und Amerikanistik, Universität Salzburg, 1979.
   Based on George R. Potter and Evelyn M. Simpson's ten-volume edition of *The Sermons of John Donne* (Berkeley: U California P, 1953–1962).

Journals

John Donne Journal: Studies in the Age of Donne. Raleigh, N.C.: English Dept., North Carolina State University, 1982–.
   Information on the journal may be found online at http://social.chass.ncsu.edu/jdj/.

Bibliographies

Alwes, Derek. "John Donne." Hager, *Major Tudor Authors,* 120–125.
    Brief biography, survey of major works and themes, critical reception, and bibliography of works by and about Donne.

Roberts, John Richard. *John Donne, an Annotated Bibliography of Modern Criticism, 1912–1967.* Columbia, Mo.: U Missouri P, 1973.

———. *John Donne, an Annotated Bibliography of Modern Criticism 1968–1978.* Columbia, Missouri: U Missouri P, 1982.

Gavin Douglas, 1475?–1522

Web Sites

"Gavin Douglas." *Representative Poetry Online.* 8 June 2003, http://eir.library.utoronto.ca/rpo/display/poet101.html.
    Selections from Douglas's translation of *The Aeneid.*

Hunter-Blair, D. O. "Gavin Douglas." *Catholic Encyclopedia.* 8 June 2003, http://www.ncwadvent.org/cathen/05143a.htm.
    A biography of Douglas reproduced from the 1908 *Catholic Encyclopedia.*

Smith, G. Gregory. "The Scottish Chaucerians." *Bartleby.com.* 8 June 2003, http://www.bartleby.com/212/#10.
    Essays on Douglas and his work from *The Cambridge History of English and American Literature,* 1907–1921. Includes a biography and commentary on his works.

Biographies and Criticism

Bawcutt, Priscilla J. *Gavin Douglas: A Critical Study.* Edinburgh: Edinburgh UP, 1976.

Bawcutt, Priscilla. "Gavin Douglas." Richardson, *Sixteenth-Century British Nondramatic Writers,* 1st ser. (Dictionary of Literary Biography 132), 112–122.

"Gavin Douglas." *Literature Criticism from 1400 to 1800* 20: 130–184.
    Excerpts of comments and criticism on Douglas from 1530–1988.

Bibliographies

Grudin, Michaela Paasche. "Gavin Douglas." Hager, *Major Tudor Authors,* 126–130.
    Brief biography, survey of major works and themes, critical reception, and bibliography of works by and about Douglas.

Scheps, Walter, and J. Anna Looney. *Middle Scots Poets: A Reference Guide to James I of Scotland, Robert Henryson, William Dunbar, and Gavin Douglas.* Boston: G. K. Hall, 1986.

Michael Drayton, 1563–1631

Web Sites

Child, Harold H. "Michael Drayton." *Bartleby.com.* 8 June 2003, http://www.bartleby.com/214/index.html#10.
The entry on Drayton from *The Cambridge History of English and American Literature, 1907–1921.* Includes a biography and commentary on his works.

"Michael Drayton (1563–1631)." *Luminarium.* 8 June 2003, http://www.luminarium.org/renlit/drayton.htm.
A comprehensive Web site on Drayton.

Renascence Editions. 8 June 2003, http://darkwing.uoregon.edu/%7Erbear/drayton1.html.
The full text of Drayton's *Endimion and Phoebe.*

"Selected Poetry of Michael Drayton (1563–1631)." *Representative Poetry Online.* 8 June 2003, http://eir.library.utoronto.ca/rpo/display/poet104.html.
Offers the full text of a selection of Drayton's poems including excerpts from *Nymphidia, The Court of Fairy,* and *Endimion and Phoebe,* as well as sonnets from *Idea.*

Biographies and Criticism

Berthelot, Joseph A. *Michael Drayton.* New York: Twayne, 1967.

Brink, J. R. *Michael Drayton Revisited.* Boston: Twayne, 1990.

Brink, Jean R. "Michael Drayton." Hester, *Seventeenth-Century British Nondramatic Poets,* 1st ser. (Dictionary of Literary Biography 121), 97–109.

"Michael Drayton." *Literature Criticism from 1400 to 1800* 8: 1–55. Excerpts of comments and criticism on Drayton from 1600–1983.

Bibliographies

Elton, Oliver, 1861–1945. *Michael Drayton: A Critical Study.* New York: Russell & Russell, 1966.

Guffey, George Robert. *Samuel Daniel, 1942–1965. Michael Drayton, 1941–1965. Sir Philip Sidney, 1941–1965.* London: Nether P, 1967.

Harner, James L. *Samuel Daniel and Michael Drayton: A Reference Guide.* Boston: G. K. Hall, 1980.

William Drummond of Hawthornden, 1585–1649

Web Sites

De Sélincourt, Hugh. "The Successors of Spenser: Drummond of Hawthornden." *Bartleby.com.* 8 June 2003, http://www.bartleby.com/214/0901.html.
A detailed essay on the life and works of Drummond from *The Cambridge History of English and American Literature, 1907–1921.*

Gillies, Valerie. "William Drummond of Hawthornden, Poet 1585–1649." *Scottish Authors.* 8 June 2003, http://www.slainte.org.uk/scotauth/drummdsw.htm.
A concise biography of Drummond from the online version of the Scottish Library Association's *Discovering Scottish Writers.*

"Selected Poetry of William Drummond of Hawthornden (1585–1649)." *Representative Poetry Online.* 8 June 2003, http://eir.library.utoronto.ca/rpo/display/poet105. html.
The full text of Drummond's "For the Baptist," "Madrigal: My Thoughts Hold Mortal Strife," "Song: Phoebus Arise," and "Sonnet: What doth it Serve."

"William Drummond of Hawthornden (1585–1649)." *Sonnet Central.* 8 June 2003, http://www.sonnets.org/drummond.htm.
A generous selection of sonnets from Drummond's 1616 collection *Poems.*

Biographies and Criticism

DiPasquale, Theresa M. "William Drummond of Hawthornden." Hester, *Seventeenth-Century British Nondramatic Poets,* 1st ser. (Dictionary of Literary Biography 121), 110–125.

Rosenblum, Joseph. "William Drummond of Hawthornden." Baker and Womack, *Pre-Nineteenth-Century British Book Collectors and Bibliographers* (Dictionary of Literary Biography 213), 93–103.

John Earle, 1601?–1665

Web Sites

"John Earle." *Wikipedia.* Ed. unknown. 22 Feb 2003. 8 June 2003, http://www. wikipedia.org/wiki/John_Earle.
A biography of Earle, originally published in the 1911 *Encyclopedia Britannica.*

Routh, Harold V. "London and the Development of Popular Literature: John Earle." *Bartleby.com.* 8 Jan 2003, http://www.bartleby.com/214/1616.html.
A brief entry regarding Earle from *The Cambridge History of English and American Literature, 1907–1921.*

Biographies and Criticism

McIver, Bruce. "John Earle." Lein, *British Prose Writers of the Early Seventeenth Century* (Dictionary of Literary Biography 151), 140–142.

Elizabeth I, 1533–1603

Web Sites

"Elizabeth I." *Kings and Queens of England to 1603.* 8 June 2003, http://www. royal.gov.uk/output/Page46.asp.
A biography of Elizabeth I from the official Web site of the British Monarchy.

"Elizabeth I (1533–1603)." *Luminarium.* 8 June 2003, http://www.luminarium.org/
   renlit/eliza.htm.
   A comprehensive Web site on Elizabeth I. Includes the full text of selected letters,
translations, and speeches, including her "Speech to the Troops at Tilbury."

"Elizabeth I: Bibliography." *Female Dramatists of the English Seventeenth Century.* 8
   June 2003, http://english.uwaterloo.ca/courses/engl710b/ElizI.html.
   A bibliography of critical works on Elizabeth I.

In Her Own Words: Elizabeth I Onstage and Online. 8 June 2003, http://www.wwp.
   brown.edu/project/rich/QEIindex.html.
   Features a chronology of the life of Elizabeth, a family tree, and a bibliography of
works on her life and times. Created by the Brown University Women Writers Project.

Marcus, Leah. "Elizabeth the Writer." Oct. 2000. *Findarticles.com.* 8 June 2003, http://
   www.findarticles.com/m1373/10_50/66157033/p1/article.jhtml.
   A helpful article by Professor Marcus on Elizabeth's speeches and poems originally published in *History Today.*

"Queen Elizabeth I of England (b. 1533, r. 1558–1603): Selected Writing and Speeches."
   Modern History Sourcebook. Ed. Paul Halsall. July 1998. Fordham University. 8
   June 2003, http://www.fordham.edu/halsall/mod/elizabeth1.html.
   Features a selection of Elizabeth's writings including her "Farewell Speech, 1601."

"Selected Poetry Of Elizabeth I (1533–1603)." *Representative Poetry Online.* 8 June
   2003, http://eir.library.utoronto.ca/rpo/display/poet112.html.
   Selected poems by Elizabeth including "On Monsieur's Departure" and "The
Doubt of Future Foes."

Biographies and Criticism

Crane, Mary Thomas. "Elizabeth." Richardson, *Sixteenth-Century British Nondramatic
   Writers,* 2d ser. (Dictionary of Literary Biography 136), 85–93.

Bibliographies

Lemmon, Rebecca. "Queen Elizabeth I." Hager, *Major Tudor Authors,* 145–149.
   Brief biography, survey of major works and themes, critical reception, and bibliography of works by and about Elizabeth I.

Sir Thomas Elyot, c. 1490–1546

Web Sites

Elyot, Thomas, Sir. "The Boke named The Governour." *Renascence Editions.* Ed. Ben
   Ross Schneider. 8 June 2003, http://darkwing.uoregon.edu/%7Erbear/gov/gov1.htm.
   The full text of Elyot's *The Governor.*

Lindsay, T. M. "Englishmen and the Classical Renascence: Sir Thomas Elyot."
   Bartleby.com. 8 June 2003, http://www.bartleby.com/213/0112.html.
   An entry on Elyot from *The Cambridge History of English and American Litera-
ture,* 1907–1921.

Biographies and Criticism

Fox, Alistair. "Thomas Elyot." Richardson, *Sixteenth-Century British Nondramatic Writers,* 2d ser. (Dictionary of Literary Biography 136), 94–106.

"(Sir) Thomas Elyot." *Literature Criticism from 1400 to 1800* 11: 56–97.
Excerpts of comments and criticism on Elyot from 1661–1983.

Bibliographies

Dees, Jerome Steele. *Sir Thomas Elyot and Roger Ascham: A Reference Guide.* Boston: G. K. Hall, 1981.

Shedd, John A. "Thomas Elyot." Hager, *Major Tudor Authors,* 150–157.
Brief biography, survey of major works and themes, critical reception, and bibliography of works by and about Elyot.

John Evelyn, 1620–1706

Web Sites

"The Diary of John Evelyn." Ed. Anthony Sallis. 19 May 2000. 8 June 2003, http://www.geocities.com/Paris/LeftBank/1914/ed_main.html.
A hypertext version of Evelyn's diary.

De la Bédoyére, Guy. "Who was John Evelyn?" Update unknown. 8 June 2003, http://www.bedoyere.freeserve.co.uk/john%20evelyn.htm.
A detailed biography of Evelyn.

"Who was John Evelyn?" Ed. unknown. 1997. British Library. 8 Jun 2003, http://www.bl.uk/whatson/exhibitions/evelynnotes.html.
Biographical information of Evelyn from a Web site supporting an exhibition on his work at the British Library.

Biographies and Criticism

Welcher, Jeanne K. *John Evelyn.* New York: Twayne, 1972.

Bibliographies

Donovan, Dennis G. *John Evelyn 1920–1968. Samuel Pepys 1933–1968.* London: Nether P, 1970.

Giles Fletcher the Younger, 1585?–1623

Web Sites

De Sélincourt, Hugh. "The Successors of Spenser: Giles and Phineas Fletcher." *Bartleby.com.* 8 June 2003, http://www.bartleby.com/214/0907.html.
An entry on Fletcher from *The Cambridge History of English and American Literature,* 1907–1921. Provides details of his life and works.

"Selected Poetry of Giles Fletcher the Younger (1585?–1623)." *Representative Poetry Online.* 8 June 2003, http://eir.library.utoronto.ca/rpo/display/poet123.html.
An excerpt from Fletcher's "Christ's Triumph after Death."

"Wooing Song." *Bartleby.com.* 8 June 2003, http://www.bartleby.com/101/233.html.
The full text of Fletcher's "Wooing Song."

Biographies and Criticism

Kastor, Frank S. *Giles and Phineas Fletcher.* Boston: Twayne, 1978.

———. "Giles Fletcher the Younger." Hester, *Seventeenth-Century British Nondramatic Poets,* 1st ser. (Dictionary of Literary Biography 121), 126–33.

John Fletcher, 1579–1625

Web Sites

"Beaumont and Fletcher: List of Plays and Poems." *Drama and Poems of Beaumont and Fletcher.* Ed. Paul Ellison. Update unknown. University of Exeter. 8 June 2003, http://www.ex.ac.uk/~pellison/BF/playlist.htm.
A complete list of the works written by Beaumont and Fletcher, both collaboratively and individually. Includes the full texts of works, including *Philaster* and *The Maid's Tragedy.*

"Fletcher, John." *Encyclopaedia Britannica Presents Shakespeare and the Globe: Then and Now.* 8 June 2003, http://www.britannica.com/shakespeare/micro/211/91.html.
A detailed biography of Fletcher. Includes bibliographies of his major works and of selected biographies and criticism.

"John Fletcher (1579–1625)." *Luminarium.* 8 June 2003, http://www.luminarium.org/sevenlit/fletcher/.
A comprehensive Web site on Fletcher.

"John Fletcher: A Biographical Sketch." *Theatrehistory.com.* 8 June 2003, http://www.theatrehistory.com/british/fletcher001.html.
A biography of Fletcher.

Macaulay, G. C. "Beaumont and Fletcher." *Bartleby.com.* 8 June 2003, http://www.bartleby.com/216/#5.
The entry on Beaumont and Fletcher from *The Cambridge History of English and American Literature,* 1907–1921. Includes biographical essays as well as discussions of their work.

"*Philaster or Love Lies Bleeding:* A Synopsis of the Play by Beaumont & Fletcher." *TheatreHistory.com.* 8 June 2003, http://www.theatrehistory.com/british/beaumont002.html.

"Selected Poetry of John Fletcher (1579–1625)." *Representative Poetry Online.* 8 June 2003, http://eir.library.utoronto.ca/rpo/display/poet124.html.
The full text of Fletcher's "Care-charming Sleep," "Hence, all you vain delights," and "Lay a garland on my hearse."

Biographies and Criticism

"Francis Beaumont and John Fletcher." *Drama Criticism* 6: 39–116.
Excerpts of criticism on Beaumont and Fletcher in general and on *Philaster, The Maid's Tragedy,* and *A King and No King* from 1940–1989, with an annotated bibliography.

"Francis Beaumont and John Fletcher." *Literature Criticism from 1400 to 1800* 33: 38–100.
Excerpts of comments and criticism on Beaumont and Fletcher from 1901–1990.

Hoy, Cyrus. "Francis Beaumont and John Fletcher." Bowers, *Jacobean and Caroline Dramatists* (Dictionary of Literary Biography 58), 3–26.

Squier, Charles L. *John Fletcher.* Boston: Twayne, 1986.

Phineas Fletcher, 1582–1650

Web Sites

De Sélincourt, Hugh. "The Successors of Spenser: Giles and Phineas Fletcher." *Bartleby.com.* 8 June 2003, http://www.bartleby.com/214/0907.html.
An entry on Fletcher from *The Cambridge History of English and American Literature,* 1907–1921. Provides details of his life and works.

"Phineas Fletcher's *Sylva Poetica* (1633)." *The Philological Museum.* Eds. M. T. Anderson and Dana F. Sutton. 1 May 1999. University of California, Irvine. 8 June 2003, http://eee.uci.edu/~papyri/sylva/.
The full text of Fletcher's *Sylva Poetica* in both Latin and English.

"Selected Poetry of Phineas Fletcher (1582–1650)." *Representative Poetry Online.* 8 June 2003, http://eir.library.utoronto.ca/rpo/display/poet125.html.
An excerpt from Fletcher's *The Purple Island.*

Biographies and Criticism

Kastor, Frank S. *Giles and Phineas Fletcher.* Boston: Twayne, 1978.

———. "Phineas Fletcher." Hester, *Seventeenth-Century British Nondramatic Poets,* 1st ser. (Dictionary of Literary Biography 121), 134–148.

John Florio, c. 1553–1625

Web Sites

"Florio's Montaigne." *Bartleby.com.* 8 June 2003, http://bartelby.com/214/0108.html.
An essay on Florio's translation of the works of Montaigne from *The Cambridge History of English and American Literature,* 1907–1921.

"John Florio (1553?–1625), writer and translator." *Decameron Web.* 8 June 2003, http://www.brown.edu/Departments/Italian_Studies/dweb/florio/florio-bio.shtml.
A short biography and a transcription of Florio's "To the Reader" from his translation of the *Decameron.*

Biographies and Criticism

Eisenbichler, Konrad. "John Florio." Richardson, *Sixteenth-Century British Nondramatic Writers,* 4th ser. (Dictionary of Literary Biography 172), 85–90.

Yates, Frances Amelia. *John Florio, the Life of an Italian in Shakespeare's England.* Cambridge: Cambridge U P, 1934.

Bibliographies

Aaron, Melissa D. "John Florio." Hager, *Major Tudor Authors,* 182–186.
    Brief biography, survey of major works and themes, critical reception, and bibliography of works by and about Florio.

John Ford, 1586–after 1639

Web Sites

"Ford, John." *Encyclopaedia Britannica Presents Shakespeare and the Globe: Then and Now.* 8 June 2003, http://www.britannica.com/shakespeare/micro/214/77.html. A concise biography of Ford.

Neilson, W. A. "Ford and Shirley." *Bartleby.com.* 8 June 2003, http://www.bartleby. com/216/#8.
    The entry on Ford from *The Cambridge History of English and American Literature,* 1907–1921. Includes biographical essays, as well as discussions of his work.

Biographies and Criticism

Anderson, Donald K., Jr. *John Ford.* New York: Twayne, 1972.

Cantor, Paul A. "John Ford." Bowers, *Jacobean and Caroline Dramatists* (Dictionary of Literary Biography 58), 91–106.

Clark, Ira. *Professional Playwrights: Massinger, Ford, Shirley, & Brome.* Lexington, Ky.: UP Kentucky, 1992.

"John Ford." *Literature Criticism from 1400 to 1800* 68: 137–256.
    Excerpts of comments and criticism on Ford from 1634–1999.

"John Ford." *Drama Criticism* 8: 127–206.
    Excerpts of criticism on Ford in general and on *'Tis Pity She's a Whore, The Broken Heart,* and *Perkin Warbeck* from 1957–1995, with an annotated bibliography.

Sanders, Julie. *Caroline Drama: The Plays of Massinger, Ford, Shirley, and Brome.* Plymouth, England: Northcote House, in association with the British Council, 1999.

Wymer, Rowland. *Webster and Ford.* New York: St. Martin's, 1995.

Bibliographies

Tucker, Kenneth. *A Bibliography of Writings by and about John Ford and Cyril Tourneur.* Boston: G. K. Hall, 1977.

John Foxe, 1516–1587

Web Sites

"The British Academy John Foxe Project." 22 June 2003. University of Sheffield. 8 June 2003, http://www.shef.ac.uk/uni/projects/bajfp/.
    From the University of Sheffield, this site features a history of John Foxe and his *Book of Martyrs (Acts and Monuments).* Additionally, the creators of the Web site plan to put up a "searchable" bibliography of works on Foxe and his *Book of Martyrs,* as well as a finding list identifying extant sixteenth-century editions of the book.

"Foxe Digital Project." The Ohio State University Libraries. Update unknown. The Ohio State University. 8 June 2003, http://dlib.lib.ohio-state.edu/foxe/.
    Features a complete facsimile of Foxe's *Rerum in Ecclesia Gestarum* (1559), as well as woodcuts images from the 1563, 1570, 1576, 1583, 1641, and 1684 editions of the *Book of Martyrs.* Also includes images of the pages portraying the stories of the more notable figures such as Anne Askew, Elizabeth I, and William Tyndale.

"John Foxe (1516–1587)." *Luminarium.* 8 June 2003, http://www.luminarium.org/renlit/foxe.htm.
    A comprehensive Web site on Foxe.

Urquhart, F. F. "Foxe's *Book of Martyrs.*" *Catholic Encyclopedia.* 8 June 2003, http://www.newadvent.org/cathen/02681a.htm.
    A concise history of Foxe and his *Book of the Martyrs* reproduced from the 1908 *Catholic Encyclopedia.*

Whibley, Charles. "John Foxe." *Bartleby.com.* 8 June 2003, http://www.bartleby.com/213/1509.html.
    The entry on Foxe from "Chroniclers and Antiquaries," found in *The Cambridge History of English and American Literature,* 1907–1921. Includes a succinct biography.

Biographies and Criticism

Highley, Christopher, and John N. King. *John Foxe and His World.* Aldershot, England; Burlington, Vt.: Ashgate, 2002.

"John Foxe." *Literature Criticism from 1400 to 1800* 14: 1–55. Excerpts of comments and criticism on Foxe from 1557–1986.

King, John N. "John Foxe." Richardson, *Sixteenth-Century British Nondramatic Writers,* 1st ser. (Dictionary of Literary Biography 132), 131–140.

Wooden, Warren W. *John Foxe.* Boston: Twayne, 1983.

Thomas Fuller, 1608–1661

Web Sites

Saintsbury, George. "Antiquaries: Thomas Fuller." *Bartleby.com.* 8 June 2003, http://
www.bartleby.com/217/1010.html.
    The entry on Fuller from *The Cambridge History of English and American Litera-
ture,* 1907–1921.

Biographies and Criticism

Sandler, Florence. "Thomas Fuller." Lein, *British Prose Writers of the Early Seventeenth Century* (Dictionary of Literary Biography 151), 157–169.

George Gascoigne, c. 1534–1577

Web Sites

Cunliffe, John W. "George Gascoigne." *Bartleby.com.* 8 Jun 2003, http://www.
bartleby.com/213/index.html#10.
    Essays on Gascoigne from *The Cambridge History of English and American Liter-
ature,* 1907–1921. Includes a biography and commentary on his works.

"George Gascoigne (1539–1578)." *Luminarium.* 8 June 2003, http://www.
luminarium.org/renlit/gascoigne.htm.
    A comprehensive Web site on Gascoigne.

"The [In]Complete Works of George Gascoigne." Ed. and update unknown, Big Wind
Press. 8 June 2003, http://leehrsn.stormloader.com/gg/.
    An online version of *The Complete Works of George Gascoigne* (Cambridge UP,
1907).

"Selected Poetry of George Gascoigne (c. 1534–1577)." *Representative Poetry Online.*
8 June 2003, http://eir.library.utoronto.ca/rpo/display/poet131.html.
    The full text of Gascoigne's "And If I Did, What Then?" "Fie, Pleasure, Fie!"
"Gascoigne's Lullaby," and "The Steel Glass."

Biographies and Criticism

Johnson, Ronald Conant. *George Gascoigne.* New York: Twayne, 1972.

Staub, Susan C. "George Gascoigne." Richardson, *Sixteenth-Century British
Nondramatic Writers,* 2d ser. (Dictionary of Literary Biography 136), 127–139.

Bibliographies

Burgess, Irene S. "George Gascoigne." Hager, *Major Tudor Authors,* 190–194.
    Brief biography, survey of major works and themes, critical reception, and bibliog-
raphy of works by and about Gascoigne.

Arthur Golding, 1536?–1605?

Web Sites

Flues, Barboura. "Arthur Golding: Brief Biography and List of Works." *Elizabethan Authors.* 8 June 2003, http://www.elizabethanauthors.com/goldBio.htm.
    Additionally, go to http://www.elizabethanauthors.com/ and scroll down to "By Arthur Golding" for a transcription of Golding's translation of *A Tragedie of Abraham's Sacrifice.*

Whibley, Charles. "Golding's Ovid." *Bartleby.com.* 6 Jan 2003, http://www.bartleby.com/214/0111.html.
    The entry on Golding's translation of Ovid from *The Cambridge History of English and American Literature,* 1907–1921.

Biographies and Criticism

Forey, Madeleine. "Arthur Golding." Richardson, *Sixteenth-Century British Nondramatic Writers,* 2d ser. (Dictionary of Literary Biography 136), 148–154.

Robert Greene, 1558–1592

Web Sites

Atkins, J. W. H. "Elizabethan Prose Fiction." *Bartleby.com.* 8 June 2003, http://www.bartleby.com/213/#16.
    Several essays on Greene and his prose works from *The Cambridge History of English and American Literature,* 1907–21.

Baker, G. P. "The Plays of the University Wits." *Bartleby.com.* 8 June 2003, http://www.bartleby.com/215/#6.
    Several essays on Greene and his dramatic works from *The Cambridge History of English and American Literature,* 1907–21.

"Greene, Robert." *Encyclopaedia Britannica Presents Shakespeare and the Globe: Then and Now.* 8 June 2003, http://www.britannica.com/shakespeare/micro/246/7.html.
    A concise biography of Greene.

"Greene's *Groats-worth of Wit.*" *Renascence Editions.* 8 June 2003, http://darkwing.uoregon.edu/%7Erbear/greene1.html.
    The full text of Greene's *Groats-worth of Wit.*

"Selected Poetry of Robert Greene (1560–1592)." *Representative Poetry Online.* 8 June 2003, http://eir.library.utoronto.ca/rpo/display/poet140.html.
    The full text of Greene's "Sweet are the Thoughts that Savour of Content," and "Doron's Eclogue" and "Sephesta's Song to her Child" from *Menaphon.*

Biographies and Criticism

Clark, Sandra. "Robert Greene." Richardson, *Sixteenth-Century British Nondramatic Writers,* 3d ser. (Dictionary of Literary Biography 167), 61–76.

Crupi, Charles W. *Robert Greene.* Boston: Twayne, 1986.

Kinney, Daniel. "Robert Greene." Bowers, *Elizabethan Dramatists* (Dictionary of Literary Biography 62), 77–93.

"Robert Greene." *Literature Criticism from 1400 to 1800* 41: 137–185. Excerpts of comments and criticism on Greene from 1882–1990.

Bibliographies

Allison, Antony Francis. *Robert Greene, 1558–1592: A Bibliographical Catalog of the Early Editions in English (to 1640).* Folkstone, England: Dawson, 1975.

Dean, James Seay. *Robert Greene: A Reference Guide.* Boston: G.K. Hall, 1984.

Hayashi, Tetsumaro. *Robert Greene Criticism: A Comprehensive Bibliography.* Metuchen, N.J.: Scarecrow P, 1971.

The Oregon Mannerists (Monica Durant, Mary A. Peters, and Kenneth R. Wright). "Robert Greene." Hager, *Major Tudor Authors,* 196–202.
    Brief biography, survey of major works and themes, critical reception, and bibliography of works by and about Greene.

Fulke Greville, First Baron Brooke, 1554–1628

Web Sites

"Fulke Greville—A Bibliography." *Fulke Greville Symposium.* Ed. Matthew Steggle. Update unknown. Sheffield Hallam University. 8 June 2003, http://www.shu.ac.uk/schools/cs/teaching/ms/projects/greville/fulkbib.htm.
    A brief bibliography of editions of Greville's works and of Greville scholarship. The main page of the Fulke Greville Symposium Site provides links to Greville related sites: http://www.shu.ac.uk/schools/cs/teaching/ms/projects/greville/fulke.htm.

"Fulke Greville, Lord Brooke (1554–1628)." *Luminarium.* 8 June 2003, http://www.luminarium.org/renlit/gfulke.htm.
    A comprehensive Web site on Greville.

Poets Corner. 8 June 2003, http://www.theotherpages.org/poems/poem-gh.html#greville.
    A selection of Greville's poems.

"Selected Poetry of Fulke Greville, Baron Brooke." *Representative Poetry Online.* 8 June 2003, http://eir.library.utoronto.ca/rpo/display/poet142.html.
    The full text of Greville's "Caelica: Sonnet 22" and the "Chorus Sacerdotum" from *The Tragedy of Mustapha.*

Biographies and Criticism

"Fulke Greville." *Literature Criticism from 1400 to 1800* 79: 65–135.
    Excerpts of comments and criticism on Greville from 1907–1992.

Gouws, John. "Fulke Greville, First Lord Brooke." Richardson, *Sixteenth-Century British Nondramatic Writers,* 4th ser. (Dictionary of Literary Biography 172), 105–115.

Larson, Charles. *Fulke Greville*. Boston: Twayne, 1980.

Larson, Charles. "Fulke Greville, First Lord Brooke." Bowers, *Elizabethan Dramatists* (Dictionary of Literary Biography 62), 94–100.

Rees, Joan. *Fulke Greville, Lord Brooke, 1554–1628; A Critical Biography*. Berkeley: U California P, 1971.

Bibliographies

Asher, Lyell. "Fulke Greville." Hager, *Major Tudor Authors,* 202–208.
    Brief biography, survey of major works and themes, critical reception, and bibliography of works by and about Greville.

Klemp, P. J. *Fulke Greville and Sir John Davies: A Reference Guide*. Boston: G. K. Hall, 1985.

William Habington, 1605–1654

Web Sites

"Habington, William." *Catholic Encyclopedia*. 8 June 2003, http://www.newadvent. org/cathen/07099a.htm.
    A concise biography of Habington reproduced from the 1908 *Catholic Encyclopedia*.

Hutchinson, F. E. "The Sacred Poets: Habington's *Castara*." *Bartleby.com*. 8 June 2003, http://www.bartleby.com/217/0215.html.
    An essay on Habington from *The Cambridge History of English and American Literature,* 1907–1921.

"Selected Poetry of William Habington (1605–1654)." *Representative Poetry Online*. 8 June 2003, http://eir.library.utoronto.ca/rpo/display/poet144.html.
    The full text of Habington's "Nox Nocti Indicat Scientiam."

Biographies and Criticism

Anselment, Raymond A. "William Habington." Hester, *Seventeenth-Century British Nondramatic Poets,* 2d ser. (Dictionary of Literary Biography 126), 133–143.

Richard Hakluyt, 1552–1616

Web Sites

The Hakluyt Society. Ed. and update unknown. 8 June 2003, http://www.hakluyt.com/.
    This site is dedicated more to exploring and travel in general than to Hakluyt. Still, helpful resources may be found in a bibliography of the publications of the society from 1847–1995.

"Richard Hakluyt." *Bartleby.com*. 8 Jun 2003, http://www.bartleby.com/214/0413.html.
    A detailed life of Richard Hakluyt from *The Cambridge History of English and American Literature,* 1907–1921.

"Project Gutenberg Titles by Richard Hakluyt." The *Online Books Page*. Ed. John Mark Ockerbloom. Update unknown. University of Pennsylvania. 8 June 2003, http://onlinebooks.library.upenn.edu/webbin/book/search?amode=start&author=Hakluyt%2c%20Richard.

The full text of works by Hakluyt.

Westfall, Richard S. "Hakluyt, Richard." *The Galileo Project*. 8 June 2003, http://es.rice.edu/ES/hurnsoc/Galileo/Catalog/Files/hakluyt.html.

A detailed outline of the life of Hakluyt by Richard S. Westfall of Indiana University.

Biographies and Criticism

Fuller, Mary C. "Richard Hakluyt." Richardson, *Sixteenth-Century British Nondramatic Writers,* 2d ser. (Dictionary of Literary Biography 136), 177–184.

Dictionaries, Encyclopedias, and Handbooks

Quinn, D. B. *The Hakluyt Handbook*. London: The Hakluyt Society, 1974.

Joseph Hall, 1574–1656

Web Sites

Hutton, W. H. "Caroline Divines: Joseph Hall." *Bartleby.com*. 8 June 2003, http://www.bartleby.com/217/0619.html.

A brief essay on Hall's theological career from *The Cambridge History of English and American Literature,* 1907–1921.

Jokinen, Anniina. "Joseph Hall (1574–1656)." *Luminarium*. 8 June 2003, http://www.luminarium.org/encyclopedia/hall.htm.

A concise biography of Hall with a bibliography of secondary works and links to Internet resources.

"Selected Poetry of Joseph Hall (1574–1656)." *Representative Poetry Online*. 8 June 2003, http://eir.library.utoronto.ca/rpo/display/poet146.html.

Contains an excerpt from Hall's *Virgidemiarum*.

Biographies and Criticism

Corthell, Ronald. "Joseph Hall." Hester, *Seventeenth-Century British Nondramatic Poets,* 1st ser. (Dictionary of Literary Biography 121), 149–162.

Corthell, Ronald. "Joseph Hall." Lein, *British Prose Writers of the Early Seventeenth Century* (Dictionary of Literary Biography 151), 174–187.

Huntley, Frank Livingstone. *Bishop Joseph Hall, 1574–1656: A Biographical and Critical Study*. Cambridge: D. S. Brewer, 1979.

Tourney, Leonard D. *Joseph Hall*. Boston: Twayne, 1979.

Sir John Harington, 1560–1612

Web Sites

"Harington, Sir John." *The 1911 Edition Encyclopedia*. Ed.and update unknown. 8 June 2003, http://58.1911encyclopedia.org/H/HA/HARINGTON_SIR_JOHN.htm.
A brief biography of Harington.

Saintsbury, George. "Sir John Harington." *Bartleby.com*. 29 June 2003, http://www.bartleby.com/213/1409.html.
A brief essay on Harington from *The Cambridge History of English and American Literature*, 1907–1921.

Biographies and Criticism

Craig, D. H. *Sir John Harington*. Boston: Twayne, 1985.

Bibliographies

Hilsman, Sarah. "Sir John Harington." Hager, *Major Tudor Authors*, 215–219.
Brief biography, survey of major works and themes, critical reception, and bibliography of works by and about Harington.

James Harrington, 1611–1677

Web Sites

"The Commonwealth of Oceana." *McMaster University Archive for the History of Economic Thought*. 8 June 2003, http://www.socsci.mcmaster.ca/~econ/ugcm/3ll3/harrington/oceana.
The full text of Harrington's *The Commonwealth of Oceana*.

Sorely, W. R. "Imaginary Commonwealths: More's *Utopia* and Harrington's *Oceana*." *Bartleby.com*. 8 June 2003, http://www.bartleby.com/217/1212.html.
An essay on Harrington's *Oceana* from *The Cambridge History of English and American Literature*, 1907–1921.

Biographies and Criticism

Downs, Michael. *James Harrington*. Boston: Twayne, 1977.

Gabriel Harvey, c. 1550–1631

Web Sites

Courthope, W. J. "The Poetry of Spenser: Gabriel Harvey." *Bartleby.com*. 8 June 2003, http://www.bartleby.com/213/1102.html.
A brief essay on Harvey from *The Cambridge History of English and American Literature*, 1907–1921.

"Gabriel Harvey." *Elizabethan Authors*. Update unknown. 8 June 2003, http://www.elizabethanauthors.com/harvey101.htm.
　　Includes a brief biography and excerpts of Harvey's verse.

"Letters from Spenser to Gabriel Harvey." *Renascence Editions*. 8 June 2003, http://darkwing.uoregon.edu%7Erbear/letters.html.
　　The full text of Spenser's side of the Spenser-Harvey correspondence published in 1580.

"Selected Poetry of Gabriel Harvey (ca. 1550–1631)." *Representative Poetry Online*. 8 June 2003, http://eir.library.utoronto.ca/rpo/display/poet149.html.
　　The full text of Harvey's "Gorgon, or the Wonderful Year" and "The Writers Postscript."

Biographies and Criticism

Erickson, Wayne. "Gabriel Harvey." Richardson, *Sixteenth-Century British Nondramatic Writers*, 3d ser. (Dictionary of Literary Biography 167), 77–93.

Shaddy, Robert A. "Gabriel Harvey." Baker and Womack, *Pre-Nineteenth-Century British Book Collectors and Bibliographers* (Dictionary of Literary Biography 213), 131–146.

Stern, Virginia F. *Gabriel Harvey: His Life, Marginalia and Library*. Oxford: Clarendon P; New York: Oxford UP, 1979.

Bibliographies

Bruster, Douglas. "Gabriel Harvey." Hager, *Major Tudor Authors*. 219–224.
　　Brief biography, survey of major works and themes, critical reception, and bibliography of works by and about Harvey.

Stephen Hawes, c. 1475–1511

Web Sites

Murison, William. "Stephen Hawes." *Bartleby.com*. 8 June 2003, http://www.bartleby.com/212/#9.
　　The entry on Hawes from *The Cambridge History of English and American Literature*, 1907–1921. Includes essays on his life and works.

"Selected Poetry of Stephen Hawes (ca. 1475–1511)." *Representative Poetry Online*. 8 June 2003, http://eir.library.utoronto.ca/rpo/display/poet150.html.
　　Provides an excerpt of "The Pastime of Pleasure."

Warren, K. M. "Stephen Hawes." *Catholic Encyclopedia*. 8 June 2003, http://www.newadvent.org/cathen/07155c.htm.
　　A biography of Hawes reproduced from the 1908 *Catholic Encyclopedia*.

Biographies and Criticism

Edwards, A. S. G. *Stephen Hawes*. Boston: Twayne, 1983.

———. "Stephen Hawes." Richardson, *Sixteenth-Century British Nondramatic Writers,* 1st ser. (Dictionary of Literary Biography 132), 166–171.

"Stephen Hawes." *Literature Criticism from 1400 to 1800* 17: 335–368.
Excerpts of comments and criticism on Hawes from 1778–1985.

Henry VIII, 1491–1547

Web Sites

"Henry VIII (1491–1547)." *Luminarium.* 8 June 2003, http://www.luminarium.org/renlit/tudor.htm.
A comprehensive Web site on Henry VIII, including the full text of selected poems, letters, and speeches.

Thurston, Herbert. "Henry VIII." *Catholic Encyclopedia.* 8 June 2003, http://www.newadvent.org/cathen/07222a.htm.
A concise biography of Henry VIII reproduced from the 1910 *Catholic Encyclopedia,* Volume VII.

Biographies and Criticism

"Henry VIII." *Literature Criticism from 1400 to 1800* 10: 113–148.
Excerpts of comments and criticism on Henry VIII from 1521–1980.

Herman, Peter C. "Henry VIII of England." Richardson, *Sixteenth-Century British Nondramatic Writers,* 1st ser. (Dictionary of Literary Biography 132), 172–186.

Edward Herbert of Cherbury, 1582–1648

Web Sites

"Edward Herbert of Cherbury (1583–1648)." *The Internet Encyclopedia of Philosophy.* 8 June 2003, http://www.utm.edu/research/iep/h/herbert.htm.
A biographical and analytical entry on Herbert.

"Edward, Lord Herbert of Chirbury (1582/3–1648)." *Luminarium.* 8 June 2003, http://www.luminarium.org/sevenlit/chirbury/.
A comprehensive Web site on Herbert.

"Selected Poetry of Edward, Lord Herbert of Cherbury (1582–1648)." *Representative Poetry Online.* 8 June 2003, http://eir.library.utoronto.ca/rpo/display/poet62.html.
The full text of Herbert's "Elegy over a Tomb."

Sorley, W. R. "The Beginnings of English Philosophy: Herbert of Cherbury." *Bartleby.com.* 8 June 2003, http://www.bartleby.com/214/1413.html.
An essay on Herbert focusing on his role in the development of English Philosophy. From *The Cambridge History of English and American Literature,* 1907–1921.

Ward, A. W. "Historical and Political Writings: Lord Herbert of Cherbury." *Bartleby.com.* 8 June 2003, http://www.bartleby.com/217/0902.html.

An essay on Herbert focusing on his political and historical writings. From *The Cambridge History of English and American Literature,* 1907–1921.

Biographies and Criticism

Bedford, R.D. "Edward, Lord Herbert of Cherbury." Dematteis and Fosl, *British Philosophers, 1500–1799* (Dictionary of Literary Biography 252), 175–181.

Hill, Eugene D. "Edward, Lord Herbert of Cherbury." Lein, *British Prose Writers of the Early Seventeenth Century* (Dictionary of Literary Biography 151), 188–197.

Norton Mary. "Edward, Lord Herbert of Cherbury." Hester, *Seventeenth-Century British Nondramatic Poets,* 1st ser. (Dictionary of Literary Biography 121), 163–176.

George Herbert, 1593–1633

Web Sites

"George Herbert." *Poets.org.* 8 June 2003, http://www.poets.org/poets/poets.cfm?45442B7C000C00010C.

A biography of Herbert from the Academy of American Poets. Also includes the full text of the poems: "The Collar," "Love (III)," and "The World."

"George Herbert (1593–1633). *Luminarium.* 8 June 2003, http://www.luminarium.org/sevenlit/her_Hlt449706632bBM_7_ert.

A comprehensive Web site on Herbert.

"George Herbert & *The Temple* Links." *George Herbert & The Temple.* Ed. unknown. 6 Apr. 2003. 8 June 2003, http://home.ptd.net/~gherbert/links.html.

A comprehensive list of links to online Herbert resources.

"George Herbert, *The Temple,* 1633." 8 June 2003, http://faculty.goucher.edu/eng211/george_herbert.htm.

Study notes on Herbert's *The Temple.*

Hutchinson, F. E. "The Sacred Poets." *Bartleby.com.* 8 June 2003, http://www.bartleby.com/217/#2.

Various essays on the life and works of Herbert from *The Cambridge History of English and American Literature,* 1907–1921. Also scroll down to the chapter "Caroline Divines" for essays on Herbert and *A Priest to the Temple or Country Parson.*

Noll, Stephen F. "George Herbert: The Country Parson." *Trinity Episcopal School for Ministry.* Update unknown. 8 June 2003, http://www.tesm.edu/Publications/Faculty_Writings/wrap.asp?doc=/old/nollher2.html.

An essay on the religious life of Herbert from Professor Noll of the Trinity Episcopal School for Ministry.

"Selected Poetry of George Herbert (1593–1633)." *Representative Poetry Online*. 8
   June 2003, http://eir.library.utoronto.ca/rpo/display/poet159.html.
      A selection of Herbert's poems including: "The Affliction (I)," "The Altar," "The
Collar," "Easter Wings," and "Love (III)."

Biographies and Criticism

"George Herbert." *Literature Criticism from 1400 to 1800* 24: 211–295.
   Excerpts of comments and criticism on Herbert from 1835–1982.

"George Herbert." *Poetry Criticism* 4: 97–136.
   Excerpts of comments and criticism on Herbert from 1694–1987, with an annotated bibliography.

Gottlieb, Sidney. "George Herbert." Hester, *Seventeenth-Century British Nondramatic
   Poets,* 2d ser. (Dictionary of Literary Biography 126), 144–167.

Stewart, Stanley. *George Herbert*. Boston: Twayne, 1986.

Indexes and Concordances

Di Cesare, Mario A., and Rigo Mignani. *A Concordance to the Complete Writings of
   George Herbert*. Ithaca: Cornell UP, 1977.
      Based on F. E. Hutchinson's edition of *The Works of George Herbert* (London:
Oxford, 1941).

Journals

George Herbert Journal. Bridgeport, Conn., 1977–.

Bibliographies

Roberts, John Richard. *George Herbert: An Annotated Bibliography of Modern Criticism, 1905–1984*. Columbia, Missouri: U Missouri P, 1988.

Mary (Sidney) Herbert, Countess of Pembroke, 1561–1621

Web Sites

"The Countess of Pembroke." *The Sidney Home Page*. 28 May 2002. University of
   Cambridge. 8 June 2003, http://www.english.cam.ac.uk/sidney/resources.htm.
      An excellent resource for Mary Sidney online. Scroll down to "The Countess of
Pembroke" for links to a detailed biography, a selected bibliography, and the full text of
her translation of *The Triumph of Death, The Tragedie of Antonie*, and "A Dialogue between Two Shepherds."

"Mary Sidney: Bibliography." *Female Dramatists of the English Seventeenth Century*. 8
   June 2003, http://english.uwaterloo.ca/courses/engl710b/sidneybib.html.
      A bibliography of critical works on Mary Sidney.

"Mary (Sidney) Herbert, Countess of Pembroke (1561–1621)." *Luminarium*. 8 June 2003, http://www.luminarium.org/renlit/mary.htm.
A comprehensive Web site on Mary Sidney.

"Mary (Sidney) Herbert, Countess of Pembroke, dedicatory poem & Psalms 52 and 139 (1595/1625)." 8 June 2003, http://faculty.goucher.edu/eng211/mary_herbert.htm.
Study notes on Mary Sidney's elegy for her brother Philip Sidney ("To Thee Pure Sprite") and Psalms 52 and 139.

"*The Tragedie of Antonie* (Ponsonby, 1595)." *Renascence Editions*. 8 June 2003, http://darkwing.uoregon.edu/~rbear/antonie.html.
The full text of Mary Sidney's translation of Robert Garnier's *The Tragedie of Antonie*.

Biographies and Criticism

Hannay, Margaret P. "Mary Sidney Herbert, Countess of Pembroke." Richardson. *Sixteenth-Century British Nondramatic Writers,* 3d ser. (Dictionary of Literary Biography 167), 184–193.

Walker, Kim. " 'Some inspired stile': Mary Sidney, Countess of Pembroke." *Women Writers of the English Renaissance.* New York: Twayne, 1996. 72–100.

Bibliographies

Alexander, Gavin. "Mary Sidney Herbert, Countess of Pembroke." Hager, *Major Tudor Authors,* 381–386.
Brief biography, survey of major works and themes, critical reception, and bibliography of works by and about Mary Sidney.

"Mary Herbert, Countess of Pembroke"; "Mary Herbert (née Sidney), Countess of Pembroke." *New Cambridge Bibliography of English Literature* 1: 1115–1116, 1468–1469, 1906.

Robert Herrick, 1591–1674

Web Sites

"The Cavalier Poets." 8 June 2003, http://athena.english.vt.edu/~jmooney/renmats/cavaliers.htm.
Brief study notes on Herrick and the Cavalier Poets.

Moorman, F. W. "Cavalier Lyrists." *Bartleby.com*. 8 June 2003, http://www.bartleby.com/217/index.html#1.
Essays on Herrick and his work from *The Cambridge History of English and American Literature,* 1907–1921.

"Robert Herrick." *Poets.org*. 8 June 2003, http://www.poets.org/poets/poets.cfm?.prmID=201.
A biography of Herrick from the Academy of American Poets. Also includes the full text of the poems "The Argument of His Book," "To Blossoms," and "To the Virgins, to Make Much of Time."

"Robert Herrick (1591–1674)." *Luminarium.* 8 June 2003, http://www.luminarium. org/sevenlit/herrick/.
A comprehensive Web site on Herrick.

"Selected Poetry of Robert Herrick (1591–1674)." *Representative Poetry Online.* 8 June 2003, http://eir.library.utoronto.ca/rpo/display/poet160.html.
The full text of selected poems of Herrick's including: "Corinna's Going a-Maying," "Delight in Disorder," and "To the Virgins, to Make Much of Time."

Biographies and Criticism

Fowler, Alastair. *Robert Herrick.* London: British Academy, 1982.

"Robert Herrick." *Literature Criticism from 1400 to 1800* 13: 308–412.
Excerpts of comments and criticism on Herrick from 1625–1988.

"Robert Herrick." *Poetry Criticism* 9: 84–148.
Excerpts of comments and criticism on Herrick from 1927–1990, with an annotated bibliography.

Rollin, Roger B. *Robert Herrick.* New York: Twayne; Toronto: Maxwell Macmillan Canada; New York: Maxwell Macmillan International, 1992.

———. "Robert Herrick." Hester, *Seventeenth-Century British Nondramatic Poets,* 2d ser. (Dictionary of Literary Biography 126), 168–181.

Indexes and Concordances

MacLeod, Malcolm Lorimer. *A Concordance to the Poems of Robert Herrick.* York: Oxford UP, 1936.
Based on F. W. Moorman's *The Poetical Works of Robert Herrick* (Oxford: Clarendon P, 1915).

Bibliographies

Guffey, George Robert. *Robert Herrick, 1949–1965, Ben Jonson, 1947–1965, Thomas Randolph, 1949–1965.* London: Nether P, 1968.

Hageman, Elizabeth. *Robert Herrick: A Reference Guide.* Boston: G. K. Hall, 1983.

John Heywood, 1497?–1580?

Web Sites

Boas, F. S. "Early English Comedy." *Bartleby.com.* 8 June 2003, http://www. bartleby.com/215/#5.
Essays on Heywood and his works, from *The Cambridge History of English and American Literature,* 1907–1921.

Early Tudor Texts. 8 June 2003, http://www.chass.utoronto.ca/datalib/codebooks/utm/ tudor.htm.
Links to the full text of Heywood's plays *The Play of the Weather* and *Gentleness and Nobility* (attributed to Heywood).

"John Heywood." *Theatrehistory.com.* 8 June 2003, http://www.theatrehistory.com/british/heywoodj001.html.
   A biography of Heywood originally published in the 1910 *Encyclopedia Britannica,* Volume XIII.

"A Praise of His Lady." *Poetry Archive.* Editor and update unknown. 8 June 2003, http://www.poetry-archive.com/h/a_praise_of_his_lady.html.
   The full text of the poem "A Praise of His Lady" attributed to John Heywood.

Warren, K. M. "John Heywood." *Catholic Encyclopedia.* 8 June 2003, http://www.newadvent.org/cathen/07319a.htm.
   A concise biography of John Heywood reproduced from the 1910 *Catholic Encyclopedia.*

Biographies and Criticism

Hayes, Edmund M. "John Heywood." Richardson, *Sixteenth-Century British Nondramatic Writers,* 2d ser. (Dictionary of Literary Biography 136), 206–213.

"John Heywood." *Literature Criticism from 1400 to 1800* 65: 269–372.
   Excerpts of comments and criticism on Heywood from 1940–1999.

Johnson, Robert Carl. *John Heywood.* New York: Twayne, 1970.

Bibliographies

Janik, Vicki. "John Heywood." Hager, *Major Tudor Authors,* 235–241.
   Brief biography, survey of major works and themes, critical reception, and bibliography of works by and about Heywood.

Thomas Heywood, 1574?–1641

Web Sites

"A funerall elegie upon the death of Henry, Prince of Wales. 1613." *Renascence Editions.* 8 June 2003, http://darkwing.uoregon.edu/%7Erbear/heywood1.html.
   The full text of Heywood's "A funerall elegie upon the death of Henry, Prince of Wales. 1613."

"Heywood, Thomas." *Encyclopaedia Britannica Presents Shakespeare and the Globe: Then and Now.* 8 June 2003, http://www.britannica.com/shakespeare/micro/270/4.html.
   A concise biography of Heywood.

Ward, A. W. "Thomas Heywood." *Bartleby.com.* 8 June 2003, http://www.bartleby.com/216/#4.
   The entry on Heywood from *The Cambridge History of English and American Literature,* 1907–1921. Includes many biographical and critical essays.

Biographies and Criticism

Baines, Barbara J. *Thomas Heywood.* Boston: Twayne, 1984.

Davison, Peter. "Thomas Heywood." Bowers, *Elizabethan Dramatists* (Dictionary of Literary Biography 62), 101–135.

McLuskie, Kathleen. *Dekker and Heywood: Professional Dramatists*. New York: St. Martin's, 1993.

Bibliographies

Donovan, Dennis G. *Thomas Dekker, 1945–1965; Thomas Heywood, 1938–1965; Cyril Tourneur, 1945–1965*. London: Nether P, 1967.

Wentworth, Michael. *Thomas Heywood: A Reference Guide*. Boston: G. K. Hall, 1986.

Thomas Hobbes, 1588–1679

Web Sites

Blanchard, Kenneth. POLS 462: Modern Political Philosophy. Course Home Page. Update unknown. 8 June 2003, http://lupus.northern.edu:90/blanchak/modern0toc.html.
Scroll down for the text of various in-depth lectures on Hobbes from Professor Blanchard of Northern State University.

"First Aid on Thomas Hobbes." Ed. H. J. Ormsby-Lennon. Update unknown. Villanova University. 8 June 2003, http://www60.homepage.villanova.edu/hugh.ormsby-lennon/HobbesFirstAid.htm.
More than just "first aid," a thorough introduction to Hobbes and his *Leviathan*.

Sorley, W. R. "Hobbes and Contemporary Philosophy." *Bartleby.com*. 8 June 2003, http://www.bartleby.com/217/index.html#12.
The entry on Hobbes from *The Cambridge History of English and American Literature, 1907–1921*. Includes various essays on his life and works.

"Thomas Hobbes." *Archive for the History of Economic Thought*. 8 June 2003, http://www.socsci.mcmaster.ca/econ/ugcm/3ll3/hobbes/index.html.
A comprehensive bibliography of scholarship on Hobbes.

"Thomas Hobbes (1588–1679): Moral and Political Philosophy." *The Internet Encyclopedia of Philosophy*. 8 June 2003, http://www.utm.edu/research/iep/h/hobmoral.htm.
A detailed biographical and analytical entry on Hobbes.

"Thomas Hobbes (1588–1679)." *Luminarium*. 8 June 2003, http://www.luminarium.org/sevenlit/hobbes/index.html.
A comprehensive Web site on Hobbes.

"Thomas Hobbes, *Leviathan*." 8 June 2003, http://faculty.goucher.edu/eng211/thomas_hobbes_leviathan.htm.
Study notes for Hobbes's *Leviathan*.

Biographies and Criticism

Condren, Conal. *Thomas Hobbes*. New York: Twayne, 2000.

McKenzie, Alan T. "Thomas Hobbes." Lein, *British Prose Writers of the Early Seventeenth Century*, (Dictionary of Literary Biography 151), 198–213.

Reilly, Susan P. "Thomas Hobbes." Dematteis and Fosl, *British Philosophers, 1500–1799* (Dictionary of Literary Biography 252), 182–194.

"Thomas Hobbes." *Literature Criticism from 1400 to 1800* 36: 106–188.
    Excerpts of comments and criticism on Hobbes from 1904–1995.

Dictionaries, Encyclopedias, and Handbooks

Martinich, Aloysius. *A Hobbes Dictionary*. Oxford, England: Blackwell; Cambridge, Mass.: B. Blackwell, 1995.

Journals

Hobbes Studies. Assen: Van Gorcum, International Hobbes Association, 1988–.

Bibliographies

Hinnant, Charles H. *Thomas Hobbes: A Reference Guide*. Boston: G. K. Hall, 1980.

Macdonald, Hugh, and Mary Hargreaves. *Thomas Hobbes: A Bibliography by Hugh Macdonald and Mary Hargreaves*. London: Bibliographical Society, 1952.

Sacksteder, William. *Hobbes Studies (1879–1979): A Bibliography*. Bowling Green, Ohio: Philosophy Documentation Center, Bowling Green State University, 1982.

Thomas Hoby, 1530–1566

Web Sites

"Baldassare Castiglione (1478–1529)." 29 June 2003, http://athena.english.vt.edu/
~jmooney/renmats/humanists.htm#castiglione.
    Study notes on Castiglioni's *The Courtier* and the English translation by Hoby.

"Sir Thomas Hoby (1530–1566)." *Luminarium*. 5 May 2003, http://www.
luminarium.org/renlit/hoby.htm.
    A comprehensive Web site on Hoby.

"Sir Thomas Hoby and Baldasarri Castiglioni [*sic*], *The Courtier*." 29 June 2003, http://
faculty.goucher.edu/eng211/hoby__castiglioni_the_courtier.htm.
    Study notes on Hoby's translation of Castiglione's *The Courtier*.

Woodward. W. H. "*Il Cortegiano* of Castiglione." *Bartleby.com*. 29 June 2003,
http://www.bartleby.com/213/1913.html.
    An entry on Hoby's translation of *The Courtier* from *The Cambridge History of English and American Literature*, 1907–1921.

Biographies and Criticism

Bartlett, Kenneth R. "Thomas Hoby." Richardson, *Sixteenth-Century British Nondramatic Writers,* 1st ser. (Dictionary of Literary Biography 132), 187–191.

Bibliographies

Hilsman, Sarah. "Thomas Hoby." Hager, *Major Tudor Authors,* 241–245.
    Brief biography, survey of major works and themes, critical reception, and bibliography of works by and about Hoby.

Richard Hooker, 1554?–1600

Web Sites

"A Learned Discourse of Justification." *Christian Classics Ethereal Library.* 8 June 2003, http://www.ccel.org/h/hooker/discourse_justification/discourse_justification.txt.
    The full text of Hooker's sermon with an introduction by James Kiefer.

"Renascence and Reformation." *Bartleby.com.* 8 June 2003, http://www.bartleby.com/213/#18.
    Essays on Hooker and his works from *The Cambridge History of English and American Literature,* 1907–1921.

"Richard Hooker (1554–1600)." *Luminarium.* 8 June 2003, http://www.luminarium.org/renlit/hooker.htm.
    A comprehensive Web site on Hooker.

"Richard Hooker (c.1554–1600)." *Ideas in Society, 1500–1700.* 8 June 2003, http://www.nd.edu/~dharley/HistIdeas/Hooker.html.
    Provides a brief biography of Hooker and bibliography of Hooker scholarship, which includes links to online articles.

"The Richard Hooker Home Page." *Trinity Episcopal Church.* Ed. and update unknown. 8 June 2003, http://www.trinitybeth.org/hooker/home.html.
    Most helpful for its "Richard Hooker Primer," a brief overview of the life of Hooker. Also provides information on new publications on Hooker.

Biographies and Criticism

Archer, Stanley. *Richard Hooker.* Boston: Twayne, 1983.

Gibbs, Lee W. "Richard Hooker." Richardson, *Sixteenth-Century British Nondramatic Writers,* 1st ser. (Dictionary of Literary Biography 132), 192–209.

Bibliographies

McGovern, Terrence. "Richard Hooker." Hager, *Major Tudor Authors,* 253–262.
    Brief biography, survey of major works and themes, critical reception, and bibliography of works by and about Hooker.

Henry Howard, Earl of Surrey, 1517?–1547

Web Sites

"Henry Howard, Earl of Surrey (1517–1547)." *Luminarium.* 8 June 2003, http://www.luminarium.org/renlit/henry.htm.
A comprehensive Web site on Surrey.

"Henry Howard, Earl of Surrey: Study Questions." 8 June 2003, http://smith.hanover.edu/sqsurrey.html.
Brief study prompts for Surrey poems, including "Love That Doth Reign," "The Soote Season," and "So Cruel Prison." Keyed to the *Longman Anthology of British Literature,* 2d ed.

"Renascence and Reformation." *Bartleby.com.* 8 June 2003, http://www.bartleby.com/213/#8
Essays on Surrey from *The Cambridge History of English and American Literature,* 1907–1921.

"Selected Poetry of Henry Howard, Earl of Surrey (1517?–1547)." *Representative Poetry Online.* 8 June 2003, http://eir.library.utoronto.ca/rpo/display/poet317.html.
Includes the full text of Surrey's "Love That Doth Reign," "So Cruel Prison," and "The Soote Season."

"Wyatt and Surrey." *Bartleby.com.* 8 Jun 2003, http://www.bartleby.com/213/1307.html.
An entry on the poetics of Wyatt and Surrey from *The Cambridge History of English and American Literature,* 1907–1921

Biographies and Criticism

Heale, Elizabeth. *Wyatt, Surrey, and Early Tudor Poetry.* London; New York: Longman, 1998.

Sessions, William A. *Henry Howard, Earl of Surrey.* Boston: Twayne, 1986.

———. *Henry Howard, the Poet Earl of Surrey: A Life.* Oxford; New York: O UP, 1999.

Bibliographies

Hulse, Clark. "Henry Howard, Earl of Surrey." Hager, *Major Tudor Authors,* 446–452.
Brief biography, survey of major works and themes, critical reception, and bibliography of works by and about Surrey.

Jentoft, Clyde W. *Sir Thomas Wyatt and Henry Howard, Earl of Surrey, a Reference Guide.* Boston: Hall, 1980.

James I (James VI of Scotland), 1566–1625

Web Sites

"James I (r. 1603–25)." *Kings and Queens of England to 1603.* 8 June 2003, http://www.royal.gov.uk/output/Page75.asp.
    A detailed biography of James I from the official Web site of the British Monarchy.

"James I and VI." *Luminarium.* 8 June 2003, http://www.luminarium.org/sevenlit/james/.
    A comprehensive Web site on James I.

"The Reign of James I." Ed. Michael Best. 8 June 2003, http://web.UVic.CA/ shakespeare-slt/history/jamessubj.html.
    A helpful introduction to the reign of James I.

Routh, Harold V. "The Advent of Modern Thought in Popular Literature: King James's *Daemonologie.*" *Bartleby.com.* 8 June 2003, http://www.bartleby.com/217/1604.html.
    A brief entry on James's *Daemonologie,* one of many Renaissance tracts concerning witchcraft. From *The Cambridge History of English and American Literature,* 1907–1921.

Biographies and Criticism

Akrigg, G. P. V. "The Literary Achievement of King James I." *University of Toronto Quarterly* 44 (1975): 115–29.

Fischlin, Daniel, and Mark Fortier (eds.). *Royal Subjects: Essays on the Writings of James VI and I.* Detroit: Wayne State UP, 2002.

Gannon, Catherine C. "James VI of Scotland, I of England." Lein, *British Prose Writers of the Early Seventeenth Century* (Dictionary of Literary Biography 151), 222–231.

Wormald, Jenny. "James VI of Scotland, I of England." Richardson, *Sixteenth-Century British Nondramatic Writers,* 4th ser. (Dictionary of Literary Biography 172), 119–135.

Bibliographies

Collier, Susanne. "King James VI and I." Hager, *Major Tudor Authors*, 266–272.
    Brief biography, survey of major works and themes, critical reception, and bibliography of works by and about James I.

Ben Jonson, 1572/3–1637

Web Sites

"The Alchemist." Public Domain Modern English Text Collection. Ed. Hugh Craig. Feb. 1995. University of Michigan. 8 June 2003, http://www.hti.umich.edu/ cgi/p/pd-modeng/pd-modeng-idx?type=header&idno=JonsoAlche.
The full text of Jonson's play *The Alchemist.*

"Ben Jonson (1572 – 1637)." *Luminarium.* 8 June 2003, http://www.luminarium. org/sevenlit/jonson/.
A comprehensive Web site on Jonson.

"Ben Jonson, 'To Penshurst' (c. 1616)." 8 June 2003, http://faculty.virginia.edu/ engl381ck/11_10.html.
Study notes on Jonson's "To Penshurst."

"Ben Jonson's *Volpone:* Issues and Considerations." Ed. Philip Mitchell. Update unknown. Dallas Baptist University. 8 June 2003, http://www.dbu.edu/mitchell/ volponeq.htm.
Study questions for *Volpone.*

"Ben Jonson." *Encyclopaedia Britannica Presents Shakespeare and the Globe: Then and Now.* 8 June 2003, http://www.britannica.com/shakespeare/micro/306/ 38.html.
A detailed biography of Jonson. Includes bibliographies of his major works and of selected biographies and critical works.

"Selected Poetry of Ben Jonson (1572–1637)." *Representative Poetry Online.* 8 June 2003, http://eir.library.utoronto.ca/rpo/display/poet179.html.
A selection of Jonson's poetry including "An Ode to Himself" and "To the Memory of My Beloved the Author, Mr. William Shakespeare."

Thorndike, Ashley H. "Ben Jonson." *Bartleby.com.* 8 June 2003, http://www.bartleby. com/216/index.html#1.
The entry on Jonson from *The Cambridge History of English and American Literature,* 1907–1921. Includes biographical essays and critical discussions of works such as *Every Man out of His Humour, Volpone,* and *The Alchemist.*

"*Volpone* by Ben Jonson." *Eserver Drama Collection.* Ed. Hugh Craig. Update unknown. University of Newcastle. 8 June 2003, http://eserver.org/ drama/volpone.txt.
The full text of *Volpone.*

"*Volpone:* Ben Jonson" and "Ben Jonson (and His Followers)." 8 June 2003, http://athena.english.vt.edu/~jmooney/renmats/volpone.htm and http://athena. english.vt.edu/~jmooney/renmats/jonson.htm.
Study notes on Jonson's life and his play *Volpone.*

Biographies and Criticism

"Ben Jonson." *Drama Criticism* 4: 222–294.
    Excerpts of criticism on Jonson in general and on *Volpone, The Silent Woman,* and *The Alchemist* from 1668–1992, with an annotated bibliography.

"Ben(jamin) Jonson." *Literature Criticism from 1400 to 1800* 6: 287–354.
    Excerpts of comments and criticism on Jonson from 1607–1987.

"Ben(jamin) Jonson." *Literature Criticism from 1400 to 1800* 33: 101–183.
    Excerpts of comments and criticism on Jonson from 1959–1989.

"Ben Jonson." *Poetry Criticism* 17: 150–220.
    Excerpts of comments and criticism on Jonson from 1964–1987, with an annotated bibliography.

Cave, Richard Allen. *Ben Jonson.* Basingstoke, England: Macmillan Education, 1991.

Donovan, Kevin J. "Ben Jonson." Bowers, *Elizabethan Dramatists* (Dictionary of Literary Biography 62), 136–182.

Evans, Robert C. "Ben Jonson." Hester, *Seventeenth-Century British Nondramatic Poets,* 1st ser. (Dictionary of Literary Biography 121), 186–212.

Kay, W. David. *Ben Jonson: A Literary Life.* New York: St. Martin's, 1995.

Summers, Claude J. *Ben Jonson Revised.* New York: Twayne, 1999.

Dictionaries, Encyclopedias, and Handbooks

Brock, D. Heyward. *A Ben Jonson Companion.* Bloomington: Indiana UP, 1983.

Indexes and Concordances

Bates, Steven L. and Sidney D. Orr. *A Concordance to the Poems of Ben Jonson.* Athens: Ohio UP, 1978.
    Based on volume III of the Hereford and Simpson edition of Jonson's works (London: T. F. Unwin; New York: C. Scribner's Sons 1893–1895; Oxford: Clarendon Press, 1954–1965).

Di Cesare, Mario A., and Ephim Fogel. *A Concordance to the Poems of Ben Jonson.* Ithaca, N.Y.: Cornell UP, 1978.
    Concords the texts in volume III of the Hereford and Simpson edition of Jonson's works (London: T. F. Unwin; New York: C. Scribner's Sons 1893–95; Oxford: Clarendon Press, 1954–1965).

Journals

The Ben Jonson Journal: BJJ. Reno: U Nevada P, 1994–.

Bibliographies

Brock, D. Heyward, and James M. Welsh. *Ben Jonson: A Quadricentennial Bibliography, 1947–1972.* Metuchen, N.J.: Scarecrow P, 1974.

Cavanagh, Sheila. "Ben Jonson." Hager, *Major Tudor Authors*, 277–285.
 Brief biography, survey of major works and themes, critical reception, and bibliography of works by and about Jonson.

Evans, Robert C., Kimberly Barron, et al. *Ben Jonson's Major Plays: Summaries of Modern Monographs*. West Cornwall, Conn.: Locust Hill P, 2000.

Guffey, George Robert. *Robert Herrick, 1949–1965, Ben Jonson, 1947–1965, Thomas Randolph, 1949–1965*. London: Nether P, 1968.

Judkins, David C. *The Nondramatic Works of Ben Jonson: A Reference Guide*. Boston: G. K. Hall, 1982.

Lehrman, Walter D., Dolores J. Sarafinski, and Elizabeth Savage. *The Plays of Ben Jonson: A Reference Guide*. Boston: G. K. Hall, 1980.

Henry King, 1592–1669

Web Sites

"Henry King, Bishop of Chichester (1592–1669)." *Englishverse.com*. Ed. and update unknown. 8 June 2003, http://www.englishverse.com/poets/king.htm.
 The full text of King's "A Contemplation upon Flowers," "A Renunciation," and "Exequy on his Wife."

"Selected Poetry of Henry King (1592–1669)." *Representative Poetry Online*. 8 June 2003, http://eir.library.utoronto.ca/rpo/display/poet186.html.
 The full text of King's "The Exequy."

Biographies and Criticism

Stringer, Gary A. "Henry King." Hester, *Seventeenth-Century British Nondramatic Poets,* 2d ser. (Dictionary of Literary Biography 126), 182–193.

Thomas Kyd, 1558–1594

Web Sites

Smith, G. Gregory. "Marlowe and Kyd." *Bartleby.com*. 8 June 2003, http://www.bartleby.com/215/#7.
 Essays on Kyd, including "Thomas Kyd's Early Work," "The *Spanish Tragedie*," "Kyd and the Early Hamlet," and "Kyd's place in English Drama." From *The Cambridge History of English and American Literature,* 1907–1921.

"Thomas Kyd (1558–1595)." *Theatre Database*. Ed. and update unknown. 8 June 2003, http://www.theatredatabase.com/16th_century/thomas_kyd_001.html.
 A concise biography and a selection of Kyd related links.

"Thomas Kyd and *The Spanish Tragedy*." Roy Underwood. Update unknown. University of West Alabama. 8 June 2003, http://facstaff.uwa.edu/rmu/kyd.htm.
 A detailed biography of Kyd, a critical discussion of his play *The Spanish Tragedy,* and a selected bibliography.

Biographies and Criticism

Braden, Gordon. "Thomas Kyd." Bowers, *Elizabethan Dramatists* (Dictionary of Literary Biography 62), 183–195.

Erne, Lukas. *Beyond the Spanish Tragedy: A Study of the Works of Thomas Kyd*. Manchester and New York: Manchester UP; New York: Palgrave, 2001.

Murray, Peter B. *Thomas Kyd*. New York: Twayne, 1969.

"Thomas Kyd." *Drama Criticism* 3: 293–338.
     Excerpts of criticism on Kyd in general and on *The Spanish Tragedy* from 1940–1976, with an annotated bibliography.

"Thomas Kyd." *Literature Criticism from 1400 to 1800* 22: 241–324.
     Excerpts of comments and criticism on Kyd from 1589–1990.

Bibliographies

Janik, Vicki. "Thomas Kyd." Hager, *Major Tudor Authors*, 294–300.
     Brief biography, survey of major works and themes, critical reception, and bibliography of works by and about Kyd.

Aemilia Lanyer, 1569–1645

Web Sites

"Aemilia Lanyer (1569–1645)." *Sunshine for Women*. Feb. 1999. 8 June 2003, http://www.pinn.net/~sunshine/march99/lanyer2.html.
     An introduction to Lanyer and her work *Salve Deus Rex Judaeorum*. Includes the introduction and apology for Eve portion of the same.

"Aemilia Lanyer." *As One Phoenix: Four Seventeenth-Century Women Poets*. Ed. Ron Cooley. 8 June 2003. http://www.usask.ca/english/phoenix/lanyera.htm.
     A biography, critical bibliography, and the full text of selected poems. The site has not been updated in some time, and some of its images are down, but the content is still worthwhile.

"Aemilia Lanyer 1569–1645." Ed. Kari Boyd McBride. Update unknown. University of Arizona. 8 June 2003, http://www.u.arizona.edu/ic/mcbride/lanyer/lanyer.htm.
     A comprehensive Lanyer site. Includes a biography, critical bibliography, and the full text of *Salve Deus Rex Judaeorum*. Home of the Early Modern Women Listserv, formerly the Lanyer List.

"Selected Poetry of Aemilia Lanyer (1569–1645)." *Representative Poetry Online*. 8 June 2003, http://eir.library.utoronto.ca/rpo/display/poet195.html.
     Includes excerpts of Lanyer's *Salve Deus Rex Judæorum*.

Biographies and Criticism

"Aemilia Lanyer." *Literature Criticism from 1400 to 1800* 30:237–268.
　　Excerpts of comments and criticism on Lanyer from 1977–1994, with an annotated bibliography.

Walker, Kim. "'This worke of Grace': Elizabeth Middleton, Alice Sutcliffe, Rachel Speght, and Aemilia Lanyer." *Women Writers of the English Renaissance.* New York: Twayne, 1996, 101–123.

Woods, Susanne. "Aemilia Lanyer." Hester, *Seventeenth-Century British Nondramatic Poets,* 1st ser. (Dictionary of Literary Biography 121), 213–220.

———. *Lanyer: A Renaissance Woman Poet.* New York: Oxford UP, 1999.

Bibliographies

Klein, Lisa Mary. "Aemilia Lanyer." Hager, *Major Tudor Authors,* 301–304.
　　Brief biography, survey of major works and themes, critical reception, and bibliography of works by and about Lanyer.

Jane Ward Lead, 1624–1704

Web Sites

Williams, George. "A Bibliography for Jane Lead." *A Celebration of Women Writers.* Update unknown. University of Maryland, College Park. 8 June 2003, http://digital. library.upenn.edu/women/lead/leadjw-bibliography.html.
　　A brief bibliography of Lead studies.

"Jane Lead, 17th Century Prophetess of God, 1624–1704." 30 Aug. 2000. *Pass the Word.org.* 8 June 2003, http://www.passtheword.org/Jane-Lead/index.html.
　　Contains a chronological, annotated index of Lead manuscripts with notes on the texts and links to the online editions.

Biographies and Criticism

Shawcross, John T. "Jane Ward Lead." Hester, *Seventeenth-Century British Nondramatic Poets,* 3d ser. (Dictionary of Literary Biography 131), 120–122.

Bibliographies

"Jane Lead." *New Cambridge Bibliography of English Literature* 2:1656–1657.

John Leland, c. 1506–1552

Web Sites

"John Leland." *Britannia History.* Ed. David Nash Ford. Update unknown. 8 June 2003, http://www.britannia.com/history/docs/leland.html.
　　A brief excerpt from Leland's "Itinerary" with an introduction to Leland's life.

Berkhout, Carl T. "Leland, John." Anglo-Saxonists—16th Century. 8 June 2003, http://www.u.arizona.edu/~ctb/16ijkl.html.
    A Leland bibliography compiled by Carl Berkhout from the University of Arizona.

Whibley, Charles. "Chroniclers and Antiquaries: John Leland." *Bartleby.com.* 8 June 2003, http://www.bartleby.com/213/1507.html.
    An essay on Leland from *The Cambridge History of English and American Literature,* 1907–1921.

Biographies and Criticism

Carley, James P. "John Leland." Richardson, *Sixteenth-Century British Nondramatic Writers,* 2d ser. (Dictionary of Literary Biography 136), 224–229.

Roger L'Estrange, 1616–1704

Web Sites

"Aesop's Fables: Sir Roger L'Estrange (1692)." Ed. Laura Gibbs. Update unknown. *Aesopica.net.* The University of Oklahoma. 8 June 2003, http://liaisons. ou.edu/~lgibbs/aesopica/lestrange/index.htm.
    The full text of L'Estrange's 1692 edition of *Aesop's Fables.*

Itoh, William H. "Roger L'Estrange, Aristocratic Publisher." Update unknown. *The History Buff.* 8 June 2003, http://www.historybuff.com/library/refestrange.html.
    An essay on the career of L'Estrange.

Trent, W. P. "Defoe: The Newspaper and the Novel." *Bartleby.com.* 8 June 2003, http://www.bartleby.com/219/#1.
    A brief biography of L'Estrange and an essay on his activity as a pamphleteer.
From *The Cambridge History of English and American Literature,* 1907–1921.

Sir David Lindsay, c. 1486–1555

Web Sites

Bawcutt, Priscilla. "Sir David Lindsay, Poet & Playwright c.1486–1555." *Discovering Scottish Authors.* 8 June 2003, http://www.slainte.org.uk/Scotauth/lindddsw.htm.
    A biography of Lindsay from the online version of the Scottish Library Association's *Discovering Scottish Writers.*

"Significant Scots: David Lindsay." *Electric Scotland.* Ed. and update unknown. 8 June 2003, http://www.electricscotland.com/history/other/lindsay_david.htm.
    A biography of Lindsay with excerpts of his poetry. Originally published in Robert Chambers's *Biographical Dictionary of Eminent Scotsmen* (1856).

Biographies and Criticism

Edington, Carol. *Court and Culture in Renaissance Scotland: Sir David Lindsay of the Mount.* Amherst: U Massachusetts P, 1994.

Parkinson, David. "Sir David Lindsay." Richardson, *Sixteenth-Century British Nondramatic Writers,* 1st ser. (Dictionary of Literary Biography 132), 233–239.

Bibliographies

Grudin, Michaela Paasche. "Sir David Lindsay of the Mount." Hager, *Major Tudor Authors,* 305–309.
    Brief biography, survey of major works and themes, critical reception, and bibliography of works by and about Lindsay.

Thomas Lodge, 1558–1625

Web Sites

Baker, G. P. "The Plays of the University Wits." *Bartleby.com.* 8 Jun 2003, http://www.bartleby.com/215/#6.
    Essay on Lodge from *The Cambridge History of English and American Literature,* 1907–1921.

Minto, William. "Thomas Lodge (1556–1625)." *Sonnet Central.* 8 June 2003, http://www.sonnets.org/minto4.htm.
    Offers a brief biography and some analysis of Lodge's sonnets. From William Minto's *Elizabethan Sonneteers* (1885).

Renascence Editions. Ed. Richard Bear. 8 June 2003, http://darkwing.uoregon.edu/~rbear/ren.htm.
    Scroll down to "Lodge" to find links to the full text of *A Reply to Stephen Gosson's Schoole of Abuse in Defence of Poetry, Musick, and Stage Plays* and *Rosalynde: Euphues Golden Legacie.*

"Selected Poetry of Thomas Lodge (1558–1625)." *Representative Poetry Online.* 8 June 2003, http://eir.library.utoronto.ca/rpo/display/poet205.html.
    The full text of Lodge's "Like to the Clear in Highest Sphere" and "Rosalind's Madrigal" from *Rosalind.*

Biographies and Criticism

Rae, Wesley D. *Thomas Lodge.* New York: Twayne, 1967.

"Thomas Lodge." *Literature Criticism from 1400 to 1800* 41: 186–216.
    Excerpts of comments and criticism on Lodge from 1914–1980.

Whitworth, Charles. "Thomas Lodge." Richardson, *Sixteenth-Century British Nondramatic Writers,* 4th ser. (Dictionary of Literary Biography 172), 136–149.

Bibliographies

Hilsman, Sarah. "Thomas Lodge." Hager, *Major Tudor Authors,* 309–315.
    Brief biography, survey of major works and themes, critical reception, and bibliography of works by and about Lodge.

Richard Lovelace, 1618–1657/8

Web Sites

"*Lucasta.*" Project Gutenberg. 8 June 2003, http://homepages.rootsweb.com/~lovelace/
lucasta.txt.
　　The full text of Lovelace's *Lucasta.*

Moorman, F. W. "Cavalier Lyrists: Richard Lovelace." *Bartleby.com.* 8 June 2003,
http://www.bartleby.com/217/0111.html.
　　The entry on Lovelace from *The Cambridge History of English and American Lit-*
erature, 1907–1921.

"Richard Lovelace." Ed. Wendy Loveless Miller. 8 Apr. 2001. *Loveless and Lovelace*
Family Official Home Page. 8 June 2003, http://homepages.rootsweb.
com/~lovelace/richard.htm.
　　A chronology of the life of Lovelace.

"Richard Lovelace (1618–1657)." *Luminarium.* 8 June 2003, http://www.
luminarium.org/sevenlit/lovelace.
　　A comprehensive Web site on Lovelace.

"Selected Poetry of Richard Lovelace (1618–1657)." *Representative Poetry Online.* 8
June 2003, http://eir.library.utoronto.ca/rpo/display/poet207.html.
　　The full text of Lovelace's "The Snail," "Song to Amarantha, that she would Di-
shevel her Hair," "To Althea, from Prison," and "To Lucasta, Going to the Wars."

Biographies and Criticism

"Richard Lovelace." *Literature Criticism from 1400 to 1800* 24: 296–355.
　　Excerpts of comments and criticism on Lovelace from 1645–1987.

Seelig, Sharon Cadman. "Richard Lovelace." Hester, *Seventeenth-Century British*
Nondramatic Poets, 3rd ser. (Dictionary of Literary Biography 131), 123–133.

Weidhorn, Manfred. *Richard Lovelace.* New York: Twayne, 1970.

John Lyly, 1554?–1606

Web Sites

Atkins, J. W. H. "Elizabethan Prose Fiction." *Bartleby.com.* 8 June 2003, http://
www.bartleby.com/213/#16.
　　Essays on Lyly and his works. From *The Cambridge History of English and Ameri-*
can Literature, 1907–1921.

"John Lyly (1554–1606)." *Luminarium.* 8 June 2003, http://www.luminarium.org/
renlit/jlyly.htm.
　　A comprehensive Web site on Lyly.

"John Lyly: *Endimion.*" Ed. Michael Best. 8 June 2003, http://www.engl.uvic.ca/
Faculty/Best/ISShakespeare/LLLCourse/lyly1.html.
A brief overview of Lyly's place in the courtly love tradition. Includes annotated
passages from his plays. Created by Professor Michael Best from the University of Victoria for his course on Shakespeare.

"Lyly, John." *Encyclopaedia Britannica Presents Shakespeare and the Globe: Then and
Now.* 8 June 2003, http://www.britannica.com/shakespeare/micro/362/7.html.
A concise biography of Lyly.

"Poems by John Lyly." *Poetry Archive.* 8 June 2003, http://www.poetry–archive.
com/l/lyly_john.html.
Includes the full text of Lyly's poems: "Cards and Kisses," "Fairy Revels,"
"Spring's Welcome," "Syrinx," and "Vulcan's Song."

"Selected Poetry of John Lyly (1554–1606)." *Representative Poetry Online.* 8 June
2003, http://eir.library.utoronto.ca/rpo/display/poet210.html.
The full text of Lyly's "Cupid and my Campaspe play'd."

Biographies and Criticism

Alwes, Derek B. "John Lyly." Richardson, *Sixteenth-Century British Nondramatic
Writers,* 3rd ser. (Dictionary of Literary Biography 167), 102–115.

Houppert, Joseph W. *John Lyly.* Boston: Twayne, 1975.

"John Lyly." *Drama Criticism* 7: 47–98.
Excerpts of criticism on Lyly in general and on *Campaspe, Sappho and Phao,* and
Endimion from 1946–1991, with an annotated bibliography.

"John Lyly." *Literature Criticism from 1400 to 1800* 41: 217–298.
Excerpts of comments and criticism on Lyly from 1890–1984.

Scragg, Leah. "John Lyly." Bowers, *Elizabethan Dramatists* (Dictionary of Literary Biography 62), 196–211.

Indexes and Concordances

Mittermann, Harald, and Herbert Schendl. *A Complete Concordance to the Novels of
John Lyly.* Hildesheim, Germany, and New York: G. Olms, 1986.
Based on the texts of the first editions of *Euphues* (1578) and *Euphues and His
England* (1580), in *The Complete Works of Lyly,* edited by R. W. Bond (1902; reprint
Oxford: Clarendon Press, 1967).

Bibliographies

Bond, R. Warwick. *The Complete Works of John Lyly, Now for the First Time Collected
and Edited From the Earliest Quartos, with Life, Bibliography, Essays, Notes,
and Index.* Oxford: Clarendon P, 1973.

Davis, Lloyd Davis. "John Lyly." Hager, *Major Tudor Authors,* 315–321.
Brief biography, survey of major works and themes, critical reception, and
bibliography of works by and about Lyly.

Christopher Marlowe, 1564–1593

Web Sites

"Christopher Marlowe." *Bartleby.com.* 8 June 2003, http://www.bartleby.com/people/
Marlowe.html.
The "Christopher Marlowe collection at Bartleby.com." Includes a brief biography, the full text of Marlowe's plays *The Tragical History of Doctor Faustus* and *Edward the Second,* as well as an essay, "Marlowe and Kyd."

"Christopher Marlowe (1564–1593)." *Luminarium.* 8 June 2003, http://www.
luminarium.org/renlit/marlowe.htm.
A comprehensive Web site on Marlowe.

The Complete Works of Christopher Marlowe: An Electronic Edition. Ed. Hilary Binda.
3 Jan. 2000. Tufts University. 8 June 2003, http://www.perseus.tufts.edu/Texts/
Marlowe.html.
Features the full text of Marlowe's complete works. Of special interest is their electronic edition of *The Tragical History of Doctor Faustus,* which includes the full text of
the two original extant versions of *Doctor Faustus,* as well as *The English Faust Book,*
which provided Marlowe with source material for his play. Created as part of the Perseus
Project at Tufts University.

"*Doctor Faustus.*" 8 June 2003, http://faculty.virginia.edu/engl381ck/10_25.html and
http://faculty.virginia.edu/engl381ck/10_27.html.
Study questions and commentary on Marlowe and his *Doctor Faustus.*

"*The Magician, The Heretic, and the Playwright:* Overview." *The Norton Anthology of
English Literature: Norton Topics Online.* 8 June 2003, http://www.wwnorton.
com/nael/16century/topic_1/welcome.htm.
A great site for students of Marlowe. Features various pages concerning Marlowe
and his *Doctor Faustus,* including explorations of scenes from *Doctor Faustus* and historical material such as excerpts from Reginald Scot's *The Discoverie of Witchcraft* and
Richard Baines' infamous testimony on Marlowe to the Privy Council. Be sure to follow
the "Explorations" link for information on "*Faustus,* Marlowe, and the English Stage."

"Marlowe, Christopher." *Encyclopaedia Britannica Presents Shakespeare and the
Globe: Then and Now.* 8 June 2003, http://www.britannica.com/shakespeare/micro/
377/43.html.
A detailed essay on Marlowe and his works. Includes a bibliography of criticism.

"Marlowe, *Doctor Faustus:* Study Questions." 8 June 2003, http://smith.hanover.edu/
sqmarlowe.html.
Study questions for Marlowe's play *Doctor Faustus.* Keyed to the *Longman Anthology of British Literature,* 2d ed.

The Marlowe Society of America (MSA). Ed. Paul Whitfield White. Update unknown.
Purdue University. 8 June 2003, http://web.ics.purdue.edu/~pwhite/marlowe/.
Provides an archive of reviews of publications on Marlowe and information on up-
coming MSA conferences. Also, as a note tells us, "The MSA newsletter is in the process
of being transferred to digital form." This resource will be a helpful addition to the site.

"Reading Questions for Christopher Marlowe's *Doctor Faustus.*" 8 June 2003, http://
english.sxu.edu/boyer/201_rdg_qsts/faustus_n7_qst.htm.
Reading questions for Marlowe's *Doctor Faustus* by act and scene.

Biographies and Criticism

"Christopher Marlowe." *Drama Criticism* 1: 211–288.
Excerpts of criticism on Marlowe in general and on *Tamburlaine, Parts 1 and II,
The Jew of Malta, Edward II,* and *Doctor Faustus* from 1946–1987, with an annotated
bibliography.

"Christopher Marlowe." *Literature Criticism from 1400 to 1800* 22: 325–402.
Excerpts of comments and criticism on Marlowe from 1820–1980.

Gill, Roma. "Christopher Marlowe." Bowers, *Elizabethan Dramatists* (Dictionary of
Literary Biography 62), 212–231.

Hopkins, Lisa. *Christopher Marlowe: A Literary Life.* Houndmills, Basingstoke, Hamp-
shire; New York: Palgrave, 2000.

Knoll, Robert E. *Marlowe.* New York: Twayne, 1969.

McAlindon, T. *"Doctor Faustus": Divine in Show.* New York: Twayne; Toronto:
Maxwell Macmillan Canada; New York: Maxwell Macmillan International, 1994.

"The Tragicall History of Doctor Faustus." *Literature Criticism from 1400 to 1800* 47:
201–408.
Excerpts of comments and criticism on Marlowe's *The Tragical History of Doctor
Faustus* from 1945–1997.

Wilson, Richard. *Christopher Marlowe.* London; New York: Longman, 1999.

Indexes and Concordances

Fehrenbach, Robert J., Lea Ann Boone, and Mario A. Di Cesare. *A Concordance to the
Plays, Poems, and Translations of Christopher Marlowe.* Ithaca, NY: Cornell UP,
1982.
Based on the text of Fredson Bowers's edition of *The Complete Works of Christopher Marlowe,* 2d ed. (Cambridge: Cambridge UP, 1981).

Ule, Louis. *A Concordance to the Works of Christopher Marlowe.* Hildesheim, Ger-
many: Olms, 1979.
Based on C. F. Tucker Brooke's *The Works of Christopher Marlowe* (Oxford:
Clarendon P, 1962).

Journals

Book Reviews, Marlowe Society of America. Waco, Tex.: The Marlowe Society of
America, 1982–.

MSAN: Marlowe Society of America Newsletter. Brookings, S.D.: The Marlowe Society
of America, 1982–.

Bibliographies

Brandt, Bruce Edwin. *Christopher Marlowe in the Eighties: An Annotated Bibliography of Marlowe Criticism From 1978 Through 1989.* West Cornwall, Conn.: Locust Hill P, 1992.

Chan, Lois Mai, and Sarah A. Pedersen. *Marlowe Criticism: A Bibliography.* Boston: G. K. Hall, 1978.

Friedenreich, Kenneth. *Christopher Marlowe: An Annotated Bibliography of Criticism Since 1950.* Metuchen, N.J.: Scarecrow P, 1979.

Johnson, Robert Carl. *Christopher Marlowe 1946–1965.* London: Nether P., 1967.

Winston, Mathew. "Christopher Marlowe." Hager, *Major Tudor Authors,* 335–342.
    Brief biography, survey of major works and themes, critical reception, and bibliography of works by and about Marlowe.

John Marston, 1576–1634

Web Sites

"John Marston (1575–1634)." Ed. Matt Steggle. Update unknown. Sheffield Hallam University. 8 June 2003, http://www.shu.ac.uk/schools/cs/teaching/ms/projects/marston/marston.htm.
    A site devoted to Marston that includes a bibliography of primary and secondary resources.

"Marston, John." *Encyclopaedia Britannica Presents Shakespeare and the Globe: Then and Now.* 8 June 2003, http://www.britannica.com/shakespeare/micro/378/35.html.
    A concise biography of Marston.

"Selected Poetry of John Marston (1575?–1634)." *Representative Poetry Online.* 8 June 2003, http://eir.library.utoronto.ca/rpo/display/poet217.html.
    The full text of Marston's "The Scourge of Villainy."

Biographies and Criticism

Bednarz, James P. "John Marston." Richardson, *Sixteenth-Century British Nondramatic Writers,* 4th ser. (Dictionary of Literary Biography 172), 155–167.

Geckle, George L. "John Marston." Bowers, *Jacobean and Caroline Dramatists* (Dictionary of Literary Biography 58), 139–168.

Ingram, R. W. *John Marston.* Boston: Twayne, 1978.

"John Marston." *Literature Criticism from 1400 to 1800* 33: 184–258.
    Excerpts of comments and criticism on Marston from 1820–1994.

Indexes and Concordances

Ward, James Xenophon. *A Concordance to "The Malcontent."* Austria: Institut für Anglistik und Amerikanistik Universität Salzburg, 1988.
Based on G. K. Hunter's edition of *The Malcontent* (London: Methuen, 1975).

Bibliographies

Pennel, Charles A., and William P. Williams. *George Chapman. John Marston.* London: Nether P, 1968.

Tucker, Kenneth. *John Marston: A Reference Guide.* Boston: G. K. Hall, 1985.

Andrew Marvell, 1621–1678

Web Sites

"Andrew Marvell." *Poets.org.* 8 June 2003, http://www.poets.org/poets/poets.cfm?prmID=312.
A biography of Marvell. Also includes the full text of the poems: "The Definition of Love," "The Mower's Song," and "To His Coy Mistress."

"Andrew Marvell (1621–1678)." *Luminarium.* 8 June 2003, http://www.luminarium.org/sevenlit/marvell/.
A comprehensive Web site on Marvell.

"Andrew Marvell 1621–1678." 8 June 2003, http://athena.english.vt.edu/~jmooney/renmats/marvell.htm.
Study notes on Marvell and his poems "A Dialogue Between the Soul and the Body," "The Nymph Complaining for the Death of Her Fawn," "To His Coy Mistress," and "An Horatian Ode upon Cromwell's Return from Ireland."

The Andrew Marvell Society. Ed. Mark Heumann. 5 Nov. 2001. St. Edward's University. 8 June 2003, http://www.stedwards.edu/hum/klawitter/scrc/marvell/marvell.html.
The Web site for the Andrew Marvell Society. The site still appears to be in its infancy, containing only information on the organization itself. Keep an eye out for possible forthcoming links to calls for papers and publications.

"Andrew Marvell, Various Short Poems, the 'Mower and the Garden' group, 'An Horatian Ode: Upon Cromwell's Return from Ireland.' " 8 June 2003, http://faculty.goucher.edu/eng211/andrew_marvell.htm.
Study notes on Marvell.

Brown, John. "John Bunyan. Andrew Marvell." *Bartleby.com.* 8 June 2003, http://www.bartleby.com/217/index.html#7.
Two essays on the life and works of Marvell from *The Cambridge History of English and American Literature,* 1907–1921.

"Marvell: 'Upon Appleton House'." Ed. Ian MacKillop. Update unknown. The University of Sheffield. 8 June 2003, http://www.shef.ac.uk/english/modules/lit207/site/imlect1.html.
A detailed analysis of Marvell's "Upon Appleton House."

"The Modern English Collection (A.D. 1500–present)." *Electronic Text Center, University of Virginia Library.* 8 June 2003, http://etext.lib.virginia.edu/modeng/modengM.browse.html.
   Scroll down to "Marvell" to find an electronic version of the 1681 edition of his *Miscellaneous Poems.*

"Selected Poetry of Andrew Marvell (1621–1678)." *Representative Poetry Online.* 8 June 2003, http://eir.library.utoronto.ca/rpo/display/poet218.html.
   A selection of Marvell's poetry, including "The Mower to the Glow-Worms, " To his Coy Mistress," and "Upon Appleton House."

Biographies and Criticism

"Andrew Marvell." *Literature Criticism from 1400 to 1800* 4: 391–451.
   Excerpts of comments and criticism on Marvell from 1756–1984.

"Andrew Marvell." *Literature Criticism from 1400 to 1800* 43: 250–328.
   Excerpts of comments and criticism on Marvell from 1957–1995.

"Andrew Marvell." *Poetry Criticism* 10: 257–327.
   Excerpts of comments and criticism on Marvell from 1921–1982, with an annotated bibliography.

Healy, Thomas. *Andrew Marvell.* London and New York: Longman, 1998.

Hyman, Lawrence William. *Andrew Marvell.* New York: Twayne, 1964.

Wheeler, Thomas. *Andrew Marvell Revisited.* New York: Twayne; London: Prentice Hall International, 1996.

Young, R. V. "Andrew Marvell." Hester, *Seventeenth-Century British Nondramatic Poets,* 3rd ser. (Dictionary of Literary Biography 131), 134–152.

Indexes and Concordances

Guffey, George Robert. *A Concordance to the English Poems of Andrew Marvell.* Chapel Hill: U North Carolina P, 1974.
   Based on H. M. Margoliouth, *The Poems and Letters of Andrew Marvell* (Oxford: Clarendon P,1952).

Bibliographies

Collins, Dan S. *Andrew Marvell, a Reference Guide.* Boston: G. K. Hall, 1981.

Donovan, Dennis G. *Andrew Marvell, 1927–1967.* London, Nether P, 1969.

Mary, Queen of Scots, 1542–1587

Web Sites

"Mary, Queen of Scots." *Englishhistory.net.* 8 June 2003, http://www.englishhistory.net/tudor/relative/maryqos.html.
   Includes a chronology and an illustrated biography.

Pollen, J. H. "Mary Queen of Scots." *Catholic Encyclopedia.* 8 June 2003, http://www. newadvent.org/cathen/09764a.htm.
　　A concise biography of Mary reproduced from the 1908 *Catholic Encyclopedia.*

The World of Mary, Queen Of Scots: Official Site of the Marie Stuart Society. Ed. and update unknown. 8 June 2003, http://www.marie-stuart.co.uk/.
　　A site devoted to Mary Queen of Scots. Includes a biography, a timeline, family trees, and examples of her poetry and prose.

Bibliographies

Collier, Susanne. "Mary, Queen of Scots." Hager, *Major Tudor Authors,* 343–345.
　　Brief biography, survey of major works and themes, critical reception, and bibliography of works by and about Mary, Queen of Scots.

Philip Massinger, 1583–1640

Web Sites

Koeppel, Emil. "Philip Massinger." *Bartleby.com.* 8 June 2003, http://www.bartleby. com/216/index.html#6.
　　The entry on Massinger from *The Cambridge History of English and American Literature,* 1907–1921. Includes various essays on his life and work.

"Massinger, Philip." *Encyclopaedia Britannica Presents Shakespeare and the Globe: Then and Now.* 8 June 2003, http://www.britannica.com/shakespeare/micro/380/ 24.html.
　　A concise biography of Massinger.

"Philip Massinger." *TheatreHistory.com.* 8 June 2003, http://www.theatrehistory.com/ british/massinger001.html.
　　A biography of Massinger, as well as information on his plays *The Virgin Martyr, The Renegado,* and *A New Way To Pay Old Debts.* From Alfred Bates's *The Drama: Its History, Literature and Influence on Civilization* (1906).

"Philip Massinger (1583–1640)." *Luminarium.* 8 June 2003, http://www.luminarium. org/sevenlit/massinger/.
　　A comprehensive Web site on Massinger.

Biographies and Criticism

Adler, Doris Ray. *Philip Massinger.* Boston: Twayne, 1987.

Clark, Ira. *Professional Playwrights: Massinger, Ford, Shirley, & Brome.* Lexington, Ky.: UP Kentucky, 1992.

Edwards, Philip. "Philip Massinger." Bowers, *Jacobean and Caroline Dramatists* (Dictionary of Literary Biography 58), 169–189.

"Philip Massinger." *Literature Criticism from 1400 to 1800* 70: 65–168.
　　Excerpts of comments and criticism on Massinger from 1920–1994.

Sanders, Julie. *Caroline Drama: The Plays of Massinger, Ford, Shirley, and Brome.* Plymouth, England: Northcote House, in association with the British Council, 1999.

Thomas Middleton, 1580–1627

Web Sites

"Dekker and Middleton, *The Roaring Girl:* Study Questions." 8 June 2003, http://smith.hanover.edu/sqroargirl.html.
Study questions for Middleton and Thomas Dekker's play *The Roaring Girl.*

"Middleton, Thomas." *Encyclopaedia Britannica Presents Shakespeare and the Globe: Then and Now.* 8 June 2003, http://www.britannica.com/shakespeare/micro/392/71.html.
A concise biography of Middleton.

Symons, Arthur. "Middleton and Rowley." *Bartleby.com.* 8 June 2003, http://www.bartleby.com/216/index.html#3.
Biographical and critical essays on Middleton from *The Cambridge History of English and American Literature,* 1907–1921.

"Thomas Middleton (c. 1580–1627)." *Luminarium.* 8 June 2003, http://www.luminarium.org/sevenlit/middleton/.
A comprehensive Web site on Middleton.

"Thomas Middleton (1580–1627)." Ed. Chris Cleary. 8 June 2003, http://www.tech.org/~cleary/middhome.html.
Features the full text of Middleton's works.

Biographies and Criticism

Brittin, Norman A. *Thomas Middleton.* New York: Twayne, 1972.

Howard–Hill, T.H. "Thomas Middleton." Bowers, *Jacobean and Caroline Dramatists* (Dictionary of Literary Biography 58), 196–222.

"Thomas Middleton." *Drama Criticism* 5: 98–179.
Excerpts of criticism on Middleton in general and on *The Revenger's Tragedy* (sometimes attributed to Middleton), *A Chaste Maid in Cheapside, Women Beware Women,* and *The Changeling* from 1927–1987, with an annotated bibliography.

"Thomas Middleton." *Literature Criticism from 1400 to 1800* 33: 259–330.
Excerpts of comments and criticism on Middleton from 1887–1991.

White, Martin. *Middleton and Tourneur.* New York: St. Martin's, 1992.

Bibliographies

Steen, Sara Jayne. *Thomas Middleton: A Reference Guide.* Boston: G.K. Hall, 1984.

Wolff, Dorothy. *Thomas Middleton: An Annotated Bibliography.* New York: Garland, 1985.

John Milton, 1608–1674

Web Sites

"John Milton (1608–1674)." *Luminarium.* 8 June 2003, http://www.luminarium. org/sevenlit/milton/.
A comprehensive Web site on Milton.

"A John Milton Chronology." Ed. Kevin J.T. Creamer. 3 Apr. 1997. University of Richmond. 8 June 2003, http://www.richmond.edu/~creamer/milton/chronology.html.
A detailed Milton chronology created by Roy C. Flannagan. Reproduced from his edition of Milton's *Paradise Lost.*

"John Milton, *Paradise Lost.* The Classic Text: Traditions and Interpretations." 19 Nov. 2001. University of Wisconsin, Milwaukee. 8 June 2003, http://www.uwm.edu/ Library/special/exhibits/clastext/clspg117.htm.
An online book exhibit from the University of Wisconsin, Milwaukee Libraries. Provides an illustrated publication history of Milton's *Paradise Lost.*

"John Milton, *Paradise Lost,* Books I and II." 8 Jun 2003, http://faculty.goucher. edu/eng211/john_miltonparadise_lost12.htm.
Study notes for *Paradise Lost,* Books I and II.

"Milton, *Paradise Lost:* Study Questions." 8 June 2003, http://smith.hanover.edu/ sqmilton.html.
Study questions for Milton's *Paradise Lost.* Keyed to the *Longman Anthology of British Literature,* 2d ed.

"*The Milton Quarterly.*" Ed. Beth Quitslund. 21 Sep. 2000. Ohio University. 8 June 2003, http://www.ohiou.edu/milton/index.html.
Home to *Milton Quarterly,* this site contains information on the journal and links to Milton and other Renaissance-related Web sites.

"Milton Reading Room." Ed. Thomas Luxon. Update unknown. Dartmouth College. 8 June 2003, http://www.dartmouth.edu/research/milton/reading_room/.
Features annotated, full text selections of Milton's poetry and prose, including *Paradise Lost* and *Paradise Regained.* Also features a selected bibliography of Milton criticism.

"The Milton-L Homepage." Ed. Kevin J. T. Creamer. 2 Mar. 2003. University of Richmond. 8 June 2003, http://www.urich.edu/~creamer/milton/index.html.
The online home of Milton-L, a discussion group devoted to Milton. This site also provides information on the Milton Society of America and the *Milton Review.* Includes a chronology and links to E-texts.

"Reading Questions for John Milton's *Paradise Lost.*" 8 June 2003, http://english. sxu.edu/boyer/201_rdg_qsts/parlost_n7_qst.htm.
Reading questions for Milton's *Paradise Lost.*

Saintsbury, George. "Milton." *Bartleby.com.* 8 June 2003, http://www.bartleby.com/ 217/index.html#5.
The entry on Milton from *The Cambridge History of English and American Literature,* 1907–1921. Includes twenty-two essays on Milton's life and works.

Siemens, R. G. "Milton's Works and Life: Select Studies and Resources." *Early Modern Literary Studies*. 8 June 2003, http://www.humanities.ualberta.ca/emls/iemls/postprint/CCM2Biblio.html.
A comprehensive Milton bibliography divided into helpful categories.

Biographies and Criticism

Blessington, Francis C. *Paradise Lost: Ideal and Tragic Epic*. Boston: Twayne, 1988.

Brown, Cedric C. *John Milton: A Literary Life*. New York: St. Martin's, 1995.

Corns, Thomas N. *John Milton: The Prose Works*. New York: Twayne; London: Prentice Hall International, 1998.

"John Milton." *Literature Criticism from 1400 to 1800* 9: 155–266.
Excerpts of comments and criticism on Milton from 1652–1988.

"John Milton." *Literature Criticism from 1400 to 1800* 43: 329–427.
Excerpts of comments and criticism on Milton from 1941–1996.

"John Milton." *Poetry Criticism* 19: 189–264.
Excerpts of comments and criticism on Milton from 1818–1993, with an annotated bibliography.

Labriola, Albert C. "John Milton." Hester, *Seventeenth-Century British Nondramatic Poets,* 3d ser. (Dictionary of Literary Biography 131), 153–189.

Miller, David M. *John Milton: Poetry*. Boston: Twayne, 1978.

"Paradise Lost." *Poetry Criticism* 29: 193–294.
Excerpts of comments and criticism on Milton's *Paradise Lost* from 1674–1995, with an annotated bibliography.

Patterson, Annabel. *John Milton*. London and New York: Longman, 1992.

Stavely, Keith W.F. "John Milton." Lein, *British Prose Writers of the Early Seventeenth Century* (Dictionary of Literary Biography 151), 232–252.

Dictionaries, Encyclopedias, and Handbooks

Bradford, Richard. *The Complete Critical Guide to John Milton*. London and New York: Routledge, 2001.

Campbell, Gordon. *A Milton Chronology*. New York: St. Martin's, 1997.

Corns, Thomas N. *A Companion to Milton*. Oxford, UK; Malden, Mass.: Blackwell, 2001.

Gilbert, Allan H. *A Geographical Dictionary of Milton*. New Haven: Yale UP; London: Humphrey Milford, Oxford UP, 1919.

Hunter, William B., Jr., et al. *A Milton Encyclopedia*. Lewisburg, Penn.: Bucknell UP, c. 1978–.

Isitt, Larry. *All the Names in Heaven: A Reference Guide to Milton's Supernatural Names and Epic Similes*. Lanham, Md.: Scarecrow, 2002.

Le Comte, Edward. *A Milton Dictionary.* New York: AMS P, 1969.
Reprint of the edition published by Philosophical Library, 1961.

Nicolson, Marjorie Hope. *A Reader's Guide to John Milton.* Syracuse, N.Y.: Syracuse UP, 1998.

Indexes and Concordances

Hudson, Gladys W. *Paradise Lost: A Concordance.* Detroit: Gale, 1970.
Based on Harris Francis Fletcher's edition of *Paradise Lost* (Urbana: U Illinois Press, 1948).

Ingram, William, and Kathleen Swaim. *A Concordance to Milton's English Poetry.* Oxford: Clarendon P, 1972.
Concords the texts of early editions, manuscripts, fragments, and variants of Milton's English poems.

Sterne, Laurence, and Harold H. Kollmeier. *A Concordance to the English Prose of John Milton.* Binghamton, N.Y.: Medieval and Renaissance Texts and Studies, 1985.
Based on Don M. Wolfe's *Complete Prose Works of John Milton* (New Haven: Yale UP, 1953–82).

Journals

Milton Quarterly. Athens: Department of English, Ohio University, 1967–.
Information on this journal may be found at http://www.ohiou.edu/milton/index.html.

Milton Studies. Pittsburgh: U Pittsburgh P, 1969–.

Bibliographies

Jones, Edward. *Milton's Sonnets: An Annotated Bibliography, 1900–1992.* Binghamton, N.Y.: Medieval and Renaissance Texts and Studies, 1994.

Klemp, P. J. *The Essential Milton: An Annotated Bibliography of Major Modern Studies.* Boston: G. K. Hall, 1989.

———. *Paradise Lost: An Annotated Bibliography.* Lanham, Md.: Scarecrow; Pasadena, Calif.: Salem P, 1996.

Patrides, C. A. *An Annotated Critical Bibliography of John Milton.* Brighton, England: Harvester, 1987.

Stevens, David Harrison. *Reference Guide to Milton, From 1800 to the Present Day.* New York: Russell & Russell, 1967.
Reprint of the edition published by the U of Chicago P, 1930. This volume is updated by Fletcher, Harris Francis, *Contributions to a Milton Bibliography, 1800–1930* (Urbana: U Illinois, 1931); Huckabay, Calvin, *John Milton, a Bibliographical Supplement, 1929–1968* (Pittsburgh: Duquesne UP, 1969); and Huckabay, Calvin, and Paul J. Klemp, *John Milton: An Annotated Bibliography, 1968–1988* (Pittsburgh, Pa.: Duquesne UP, 1996).

Henry More, 1614–1687

Web Sites

Hutton, Sarah. "The Cambridge Platonists." *Stanford Encyclopedia of Philosophy*. 8 June 2003, http://plato.stanford.edu/entries/cambridge-platonists/.
An essay on the More and the Cambridge Platonists. Includes a selected bibliography of primary and secondary resources.

O'Connor , J. J., and E. F. Robertson. "Henry More." *The MacTutor History of Mathematics Archive*. Apr. 2002. University of St. Andrews. 2 May 2003, http://www-gap.dcs.st-and.ac.uk/~history/Mathematicians/More_Henry.html.
A concise biography of More.

Westfall, Richard S. "More, Henry." *The Galileo Project*. 8 June 2003, http://es.rice.edu/ES/humsoc/Galileo/Catalog/Files/more.html.
A detailed outline of the life of More by Richard S. Westfall of Indiana University.

Biographies and Criticism

"Henry More." *Literature Criticism from 1400 to 1800* 9: 290–332.
Excerpts of comments and criticism on More from 1687–1985.

Hutton, Sarah. "Henry More." Dematteis and Fosl, *British Philosophers, 1500–1799* (Dictionary of Literary Biography 252), 264–273.

Hutton, Sarah, and Robert Crocker. *Henry More (1614–1687) Tercentenary Studies*. Dordrecht, The Netherlands; Boston: Kluwer Academic, 1990.

Klawitter, George. "Henry More." Hester, *Seventeenth-Century British Nondramatic Poets,* 2d ser. (Dictionary of Literary Biography 126), 211–221.

Sir Thomas More, 1477?–1535

Web Sites

The Center for Thomas More Studies. Ed. and update unknown. The University of Dallas. 8 June 2003, http://www.thomasmorestudies.org/.
The Web site of the Center for Thomas More Studies at the University of Dallas. Features a biography, chronology, curriculum materials for teachers, and the full text of More's works and relevant historical documents,

Hudleston, G. Roger. "St. Thomas More." *Catholic Encyclopedia*. 8 June 2003, http://www.newadvent.org/cathen/14689c.htm.
A detailed biography of More reproduced from the 1912 *Catholic Encyclopedia,* Vol. XIV.

Lakowski, Romuald Ian. "Thomas More Bibliography (Part A)" and "Thomas More Bibliography (Part B)." *Early Modern Literary Studies*. 8 June 2003, http://www.shu.ac.uk/emls/iemls/work/chapters/morebib1.html and http://www.shu.ac.uk/emls/iemls/work/chapters/morebib2.html.
An exhaustive bibliography of Thomas More.

———. "Summary of *Utopia,* Book I and Conclusion to Book II." *Early Modern Literary Studies.* 8 June 2003, http://www.humanities.ualberta.ca/emls/iemls/work/chapters/utopsum.html.
A helpful overview of Book I of *Utopia.*

Renascence Editions. Ed. Richard Bear. 8 June 2003, http://darkwing.uoregon.edu/~rbear/ren.htm.
Contains the full text of Thomas More's *The History of King Richard the Third* and William Roper's *The Mirrour of Vertue in Worldly Greatnes; or The Life of Sir Thomas More.*

"Sir Thomas More." *Luminarium.* 8 June 2003, http://www.luminarium.org/renlit/tmore.htm.
A comprehensive Web site on More.

"Sir Thomas More and *Utopia.*" 8 June 2003, http://faculty.goucher.edu/eng211/sir_thomas_more__utopia.htm.
Study notes on More's *Utopia.*

"Thomas More & His *Utopia* (ca 1478–1535)." 8 June 2003, http://athena.english.vt.edu/~jmooney/renmats/more.htm.
An introduction to More and his *Dialogues* and *Utopia.*

Thomas More Website. Ed. W. David Holliday. 8 May 2003. 8 June 2003, http://www.d-holliday.com/tmore/.
An extensive site that includes a biography, chronology, bibliography, a directory of More societies, and a page of More links.

Biographies and Criticism

Fox, Alistair. *Utopia: An Elusive Vision.* New York: Twayne; Toronto: Maxwell Macmillan Canada; New York: Maxwell Macmillan International, 1993.

McCutcheon, Elizabeth. "Sir Thomas More." Richardson, *Sixteenth-Century British Nondramatic Writers,* 2d ser. (Dictionary of Literary Biography 136), 235–254.

"Thomas More." *Literature Criticism from 1400 to 1800* 10: 353–456.
Excerpts of comments and criticism on More from 1516–1984.

"Utopia." *Literature Criticism from 1400 to 1800* 32: 252–359.
Excerpts of comments and criticism on More's *Utopia* from 1867–1992.

Indexes and Concordances

Bolchazy, Ladislaus J., Gregory Gichan, and Frederick Theobald. *A Concordance to the Utopia of St. Thomas More and a Frequency Word List.* Hildesheim, Germany, and New York: Georg Olms, 1978.
Based on Edward Surtz, S. J. Hexter, and J. H. Hexter's *Yale Edition of the Complete Works of St. Thomas More, Volume 4* (New Haven: Yale UP, 1965).

Journals

Moreana. Angers Cedex, France: Association Amici Thomae Mori, 1963–.

Bibliographies

Boswell, Jackson Campbell. *Sir Thomas More in the English Renaissance: An Anno-tated Catalogue.* Binghamton, N.Y.: Medieval and Renaissance Texts and Studies, 1994.

Geritz, Albert J. *Thomas More: An Annotated Bibliography of Criticism, 1935–1997.* Westport, Conn.: Greenwood P, 1998.

Gibson, R. W., and J. Max Patrick. *St. Thomas More: A Preliminary Bibliography of His Works and of Moreana to the Year 1750.* New Haven: Yale UP, 1961.
    Updated by Smith, Constance, *An Updating of R.W. Gibson's St. Thomas More, a Preliminary Bibliography* (St. Louis: Center for Reformation Research, 1981).

Hardin, Richard F. "Thomas More." Hager, *Major Tudor Authors,* 351–358.
    Brief biography, survey of major works and themes, critical reception, and bibliog-raphy of works by and about More.

Wentworth, Michael D. *The Essential Sir Thomas More: An Annotated Bibliography of Major Modern Studies.* New York: G. K. Hall, 1995.

Richard Mulcaster, c. 1531–1611

Web Sites

"Richard Mulcaster." Ed. and update unknown. Merchant Taylor's School. 8 June 2003, http://www.mtsn.org.uk/about/mulcastr.htm.
    A concise biography of Mulcaster from the Web site of the Merchant Taylor's School, where he served as headmaster.

"Richard Mulcaster: *Positions Concerning the Training Up of Children* (1581)." Ed. William Barker. Update unknown. Memorial University of Newfoundland. 8 June 2003, http://www.ucs.mun.ca/~wbarker/positions.html.
    The full text of Mulcaster's *Positions Concerning the Training Up of Children* with an introduction by Professor Barker of Memorial University of Newfoundland.

Woodward, W. H. "English Universities, Schools and Scholarship in the Sixteenth Cen-tury: Richard Mulcaster." *Bartleby.com.* 8 June 2003, http://www.bartleby.com/213/1912.html.
    An entry on Mulcaster from *The Cambridge History of English and American Lit-erature,* 1907–1921.

Biographies and Criticism

Barker, William. "Richard Mulcaster." Richardson, *Sixteenth-Century British Nondramatic Writers,* 3d ser. (Dictionary of Literary Biography 167), 134—141.

Anthony Munday, 1560–1633

Web Sites

"Anthony Munday: Elizabethan Prose Fiction." *Bartleby.com.* 8 June 2003, http://www.
bartleby.com/213/1616.html.
A brief entry on Munday's prose writing from *The Cambridge History of English
and American Literature, 1907–1921.*

"The Downfall of Robert, Earle of Huntington and *The Death of Robert, Earle of Hunting-
ton:* Introduction." *Teams Middle English Texts.* Ed. Russell Peck. Update unknown.
University of Rochester and Western Michigan University, Kalamazoo, Michigan. 8
June 2003, http://www.lib.rochester.edu/camelot/teams/dowdeint.htm.
Contains the full text of Munday's two Robin Hood plays, taken from Stephen
Knight and Thomas H. Ohlgren's edition *Robin Hood and Other Outlaw Tales*
(Kalamazoo, Mich.: Medieval Institute Publications, 1997). Includes an introduction to
the texts.

"Lesser Elizabethan Dramatists: Anthony Munday's career (1553–1633) and industry as
a writer." *Bartleby.com.* 8 June 2003, http://www.bartleby.com/215/1303.html.
A concise entry on Munday's dramatic writing from *The Cambridge History of
English and American Literature, 1907–1921.*

"Munday, Anthony." *Encyclopaedia Britannica Presents Shakespeare and the Globe:
Then and Now.* 8 June 2003, http://www.britannica.com/shakespeare/micro/
409/91.html.
A concise biography of Munday.

"Selected Poetry of Anthony Munday (1560–1633)." *Representative Poetry Online.* 8
June 2003, http://eir.library.utoronto.ca/rpo/display/poet238.html.
Contains the full text of "Beauty Sat Bathing by a Spring" attributed to Munday.

Biographies and Criticism

Ayres, Philip J. "Anthony Munday." Bowers, *Elizabethan Dramatists* (Dictionary of
Literary Biography 62), 232–241.

Branyan, Richard H. "Anthony Munday." Richardson, *Sixteenth-Century British
Nondramatic Writers,* 4th ser. (Dictionary of Literary Biography 172), 173–180.

Thomas Nashe, 1567–1601

Web Sites

Atkins, J. W. H. "Elizabethan Prose Fiction." *Bartleby.com.* 8 June 2003, http://www.
bartleby.com/213/#16.
Entries on Nashe from *The Cambridge History of English and American Literature, 1907–1921.* Includes a biography and several essays on his work, including *The
Unfortunate Traveller.*

"Nashe, Thomas." *Encyclopaedia Britannica Presents Shakespeare and the Globe: Then and Now.* 8 June 2003, http://www.britannica.com/shakespeare/micro/416/21.html.
    A concise biography of Nashe.

"Selected Poetry of Thomas Nashe (1567–1601)." *Representative Poetry Online.* 8 June 2003, http://eir.library.utoronto.ca/rpo/display/poet239.html.
    Contains the full text of Nashe's "Adieu, farewell earth's bliss" and "Spring, the sweet spring."

"Thomas Nashe (1567–1601)." *Luminarium.* 8 June 2003, http://www.luminarium.org/renlit/nashe.htm.
    A comprehensive Web site on Nashe.

Thomas Nashe, Elizabethan Writer (1567 – ?1601). Ed. R. Lamb. 2 November 2001. 8 June 2003, http://members.tripod.com/sicttasd/.
    A comprehensive site on Nashe. Includes a biography, information on his works, a timeline, a bibliography, and a transcription of contemporary documents referring to Nashe.

Biographies and Criticism

Barbour, Reid. "Thomas Nashe." Richardson, *Sixteenth-Century British Nondramatic Writers,* 3d ser. (Dictionary of Literary Biography 167), 142–159.

Hibbard, G. R. *Thomas Nashe: A Critical Introduction.* Cambridge: Harvard UP, 1962.

McGinn, Donald Joseph. *Thomas Nashe.* Boston: Twayne, 1981.

"Thomas Nashe." *Literature Criticism from 1400 to 1800* 41: 299–388.
    Excerpts of comments and criticism on Nashe from 1890–1994.

Indexes and Concordances

Ule, Louis. *A Concordance to the Works of Thomas Nashe.* Hildesheim, Germany, and New York: Olms, 1997.
    Based on R. B. McKerrow's edition of *The Works of Thomas Nashe* (London: A. H. Bullen, 1904–1910).

Bibliographies

Alwes, Derek. "Thomas Nashe." Hager, *Major Tudor Authors,* 359–365.
    Brief biography, survey of major works and themes, critical reception, and bibliography of works by and about Nashe.

Thomas Norton, 1532–1584

Web Sites

Cunliffe, John W. "Early English Tragedy: *Gorboduc* and its political significance: its advance on Senecan Tragedy and early Tragicomedy." *Bartleby.com.* 8 June 2003, http://www.bartleby.com/215/0408.html.

An essay on Norton and Thomas Sackville's *Gorboduc*. From *The Cambridge History of English and American Literature,* 1907–1921.

"*Gorboduc.*" Ed. Michael Best. 8 June 2003, http://web.uvic.ca/shakespeare/Library/SLTnoframes/drama/gorboduc.html.
A page providing brief information on Norton and Sackville's *Gorboduc.*

Biographies and Criticism

Cauthen, Irby B., Jr. "Thomas Sackville and Thomas Norton." Bowers, *Elizabethan Dramatists* (Dictionary of Literary Biography 62), 261–266.

George Peele, 1556–1596

Web Sites

"George Peele." *Bartleby.com.* 8 June 2003, http://www.bartleby.com/215/0609.html.
A brief essay on Peele from *The Cambridge History of English and American Literature,* 1907–1921.

"George Peele." *TheatreHistory.com.* 3 June 2003, http://www.theatrehistory.com/british/peele001.html.
A brief biography of Peele

"Peele, George." *Encyclopaedia Britannica Presents Shakespeare and the Globe: Then and Now.* 8 June 2003, http://www.britannica.com/shakespeare/micro/456/97.html.
A concise biography of Peele.

"*Selected Poetry Of George Peele* (1556–1596)." *Representative Poetry Online.* 8 June 2003, http://eir.library.utoronto.ca/rpo/display/poet254.html.
The full text of Peele's "His Golden Locks Time hath to Silver Turn'd."

Biographies and Criticism

Braunmuller, A. R. *George Peele.* Boston: Twayne, 1983.

Horne, David Hamilton. *The Life and Minor works of George Peele.* Westport, Conn.: Greenwood P, 1978.
Reprint of *The Life and Minor Works of George Peele.* New Haven: Yale UP, 1952.

Kozikowski, Stanley J. "George Peele." Bowers, *Elizabethan Dramatists* (Dictionary of Literary Biography 62), 242–253.

Whitworth, Charles. "George Peele." Richardson, *Sixteenth-Century British Nondramatic Writers* 3d ser. (Dictionary of Literary Biography 167), 165–170.

Bibliographies

Wilson, John. "George Peele." Hager, *Major Tudor Authors,* 376–380.
Brief biography, survey of major works and themes, critical reception, and bibliography of works by and about Peele.

Katherine Philips, 1631–1664

Web Sites

"Katherine Philips (1632–1664)." *The Penn State Archive of Women Writing Before 1800.* Ed. Kathleen Nulton Kemmerer. 27 Apr. 2001. Penn State University. 8 June 2003, http://www.hn.psu.edu/Faculty/KKemmerer/18thc/women/Philips/default.htm.
The full text of "In memory of that excellent person Mrs. Mary Lloyd," "On the Fair Weather just at the Coronation," and "To Her Royal Highness the Duchess of York."

"Katherine Philips." *As One Phoenix: Four Seventeenth-Century Women Poets.* Ed. Ron Cooley. U of Saskatchewan. 8 June 2003, http://www.usask.ca/english/phoenix/philipsk.htm.
Provides a biography, bibliography, and selected poems.

"Katherine Philips: Study Questions." 8 June 2003, http://smith.hanover.edu/sqphilips.html.
Study prompts for Philips's "Friendship in Emblem," "Upon the Double Murder of King Charles," "On the Third of September, 1651," "To the truly Noble and Obliging Mrs. Anne Owen," "To Mrs. Mary Awbrey at Parting," "To My Excellent Lucasia, on Our Friendship," and "The World." Keyed to the *Longman Anthology of British Literature*, 2d ed.

North, Alix. "Katherine Fowler Philips, 1631–1664." *Isle of Lesbos.* Update unknown. 8 June 2003, http://www.sappho.com/poetry/k_philip.html.
A biography of Philips and the full text of "Friendships Mystery, To My Dearest Lucasia" and "To My Excellent Lucasia, on Our Friendship."

"Renaissance Women Online (RWO)." *The Brown University Women Writers Project.* 8 June 2003, http://textbase.wwp.brown.edu:1084/dynaweb/wwptextbase/wwpRWO/.
Scroll down to "Philips" for links to the full text of *Poems* (1664) and *Poems by the Most Deservedly Admired Mrs. Katherine Philips* (1667).

"Selected Poetry of Katherine Philips (1631–1664)." *Representative Poetry Online.* 8 June 2003, http://eir.library.utoronto.ca/rpo/display/poet258.html.
The full text of Philips's "Epitaph on her Son H. P.," "Friendship's Mystery, To my Dearest Lucasia," "Orinda upon Little Hector Philips," and "To Mrs. M. A. at Parting."

Biographies and Criticism

Hageman, Elizabeth H. "Katherine Philips." Hester, *Seventeenth-Century British Nondramatic Poets,* 3d ser. (Dictionary of Literary Biography 131), 202–214.

Thomas, Patrick. *Katherine Philips ("Orinda").* Cardiff: U Wales P, on behalf of the Welsh Arts Council, 1988.

Bibliographies

"Katherine Philips." *New Cambridge Bibliography of English Literature,* vol. 2, 480.

George Puttenham, c. 1529–1591

Web Sites

"*The Arte of English Poesie* (Attributed to George Puttenham)." *Representative Poetry Online.* 8 June 2003, http://eir.library.utoronto.ca/rpo/display/poet270.html.
The complete text of *The Arte of English Poesie.*

Atkins, J. W. H. "*The Arte of English Poesie.*" *Bartleby.com.* 8 June 2003, http://www.bartleby.com/213/1408.html.
An overview of *The Arte of English Poesie* from "Elizabethan Criticism," in *The Cambridge History of English and American Literature,* 1907–1921.

Bibliographies

"George Puttenham." Hager, *Major Tudor Authors,* 386–390.
A brief biography, survey of major works and themes, critical reception, and bibliography of works by and about Puttenham.

Francis Quarles, 1592–1644

Web Sites

"Francis Quarles (1592–1644)." *Luminarium.* 8 June 2003, http://www.luminarium.org/sevenlit/quarles/.
A comprehensive Web site on Quarles.

Hutchinson, F. E. "The Sacred Poets: Quarles and emblem poetry." *Bartleby.com.* 8 June 2003, http://www.bartleby.com/217/0216.html.
An essay on Quarles from *The Cambridge History of English and American Literature,* 1907–1921.

"Selected Poetry of Francis Quarles (1592–1644)." *Representative Poetry Online.* 8 June 2003, http://eir.library.utoronto.ca/rpo/display/poet271.html.
The full text of Quarles's "A Good Night" and "Why dost thou Shade thy Lovely Face?"

Biographies and Criticism

Roberts, Lorraine M. "Francis Quarles." Hester, *Seventeenth-Century British Nondramatic Poets,* 2d ser. (Dictionary of Literary Biography 126), 227–238.

Sir Walter Ralegh [Raleigh], 1554–1618

Web Sites

Creighton, Louise. "Sir Walter Ralegh." *Bartleby.com.* 8 June 2003, http://www.bartleby.com/214/#3.
Links to essays on Ralegh and his works. From *The Cambridge History of English and American Literature,* 1907–1921.

"Selected Poetry of Sir Walter Ralegh (ca. 1552–1618)." *Representative Poetry Online.* 8 June 2003, http://eir.library.utoronto.ca/rpo/display/poet272.html.
Full text of Ralegh's "As You Came from the Holy Land," "The Nymph's Reply," "The Passionate Man's Pilgrimage," and "Prais'd be Diana's Fair and Harmless Light."

"Sir Walter Ralegh." *English 201.* Eds. Jane Magrath and Julie Dennison. Update unknown. University of Prince Edward Island. 8 June 2003, http://www.upei.ca/english/201/sixteenth/raleigh.html.
A good collection of Ralegh-related links organized into the following categories: primary texts, biography, and criticism.

"Sir Walter Ralegh (1552–1618)." *Luminarium.* 8 June 2003, http://www.luminarium.org/renlit/ralegh.htm.
A comprehensive Web site on Ralegh.

Biographies and Criticism

May, Steven W. *Sir Walter Ralegh.* Boston: Twayne, 1989.

Mills, Jerry Leath. "Sir Walter Ralegh." Richardson, *Sixteenth-Century British Nondramatic Writers,* 4th ser. (Dictionary of Literary Biography 172), 200–216.

"Sir Walter Raleigh." *Poetry Criticism* 31: 199–319.
Excerpts of comments and criticism on Ralegh from 1930–1996, with an annotated bibliography.

"Walter Raleigh." *Literature Criticism from 1400 to 1800* 31: 220–307.
Excerpts of comments and criticism on Ralegh from 1951–1991.

"Walter Raleigh." *Literature Criticism from 1400 to 1800* 39: 71–137.
Excerpts of comments and criticism on Ralegh from 1938–1987.

Bibliographies

Armitage, Christopher M. *Sir Walter Ralegh, an Annotated Bibliography.* Chapel Hill: U of North Carolina P, published for America's Four Hundredth Anniversary Committee, 1987.

Harris, Ronald W. "Sir Walter Ralegh." Hager, *Major Tudor Authors,* 391–397.
Brief biography, survey of major works and themes, critical reception, and bibliography of works by and about Ralegh.

Mills, Jerry Leath. *Sir Walter Ralegh: A Reference Guide.* Boston: G. K. Hall, 1986.

Tonkin, Humphrey. *Sir Walter Raleigh, 1900–1968.* London: Nether P, 1971.

Thomas Randolph, 1605–1635

Web Sites

Bayne, Ronald. "Lesser Jacobean and Caroline Dramatists." *Bartleby.com.* 8 June 2003, http://www.bartleby.com/216/#9.
Includes essays on Randolph life and works: "Thomas Randolph's University training; His *Aristippus* and *The Conceited Pedler*," "Aristotle's Ethics dramatised in

The Muses Looking-Glasse," and "Originality of Randolph." From *The Cambridge History of English and American Literature,* 1907–1921.

"Selected Poetry of Thomas Randolph (1605–1635)." *Representative Poetry Online.* 8 June 2003, http://eir.library.utoronto.ca/rpo/display/poet274.html.
 The full text of Randolph's "An Ode to Master Anthony Stafford, to Hasten him into the Country" and "On Six Cambridge Lasses Bathing Themselves."

Biographies and Criticism

Kovich, Charles M. "Thomas Randolph." Hester, *Seventeenth-Century British Nondramatic Poets,*2d ser. (Dictionary of Literary Biography 126), 239–245.

Levenson, Jill L. "Thomas Randolph." Bowers, *Jacobean and Caroline Dramatists* (Dictionary of Literary Biography 58), 231–240.

Bibliographies

Guffey, George Robert. *Robert Herrick, 1949–1965, Ben Jonson, 1947–1965, Thomas Randolph, 1949–1965.* London: Nether P, 1968.

William Rowley, 1585?–1626

Web Sites

"*The Birth of Merlin: Or The Childe hath found his Father,* ascribed to William Rowley." *The Camelot Project.* Eds. Alan Lupack and Barbara Tepa Lupack. 19 June 2003. The University of Rochester. 8 June 2003, http://www.lib.rochester.edu/camelot/rowley.htm.
 The full text of the play *The Birth of Merlin,* ascribed to Rowley.

"Rowley, William." *Encyclopaedia Britannica Presents Shakespeare and the Globe: Then and Now.* 8 June 2003, http://www.britannica.com/shakespeare/micro/511/98.html.
 A concise biography of Rowley.

Symons, Arthur. "Middleton and Rowley." *Bartleby.com.* 8 June 2003, http://www.bartleby.com/216/index.html#3.
 Biographical and critical essays on Rowley from *The Cambridge History of English and American Literature,* 1907–1921.

Biographies and Criticism

Howard-Hill, T.H. "William Rowley." Bowers, *Jacobean and Caroline Dramatists* (Dictionary of Literary Biography 58), 241–248.

Charles Sackville, Lord Buckhurst, Sixth Earl of Dorset, 1638–1706

Web Sites

Johnson, Samuel. "The Life of Charles Sackville." *The Penn State Archive of Samuel Johnson's Lives of the Poets.* 8 June 2003, http://www.hn.psu.edu/faculty/kkemmerer/poets/sackville/default.htm.
The full text of Johnson's biography of Sackville.

"Selected Poetry of Charles Sackville, Earl of Dorset (1638–1706)." *Representative Poetry Online.* 8 June 2003, http://eir.library.utoronto.ca/rpo/display/poet285.html.
The full text of "Song, Written at Sea." Includes biographical information.

Whibley, Charles. "The Court Poets." *Bartleby.com.* 8 June 2003, http://www.bartleby.com/218/#8.
Essays on Sackville and the Court Poets from *The Cambridge History of English and American Literature,* 1907–1921.

Biographies and Criticism

Gill, James E. "Charles Sackville, Lord Buckhurst, Earl of Dorset and Middlesex." Hester, *Seventeenth-Century British Nondramatic Poets*: 3d ser. (Dictionary of Literary Biography 131), 73–80.

Thomas Sackville, First Earl of Dorset, Baron Buckhurst, 1536–1608

Web Sites

Cunliffe, John W. "Early English Tragedy: *Gorboduc* and Its Political Significance: Its Advance on Senecan Tragedy and Early Tragicomedy." *Bartleby.com.* 8 June 2003, http://www.bartleby.com/215/0408.html.
An essay on Sackville and Thomas Norton's *Gorboduc* from *The Cambridge History of English and American Literature,* 1907–1921.

"*Gorboduc*." Ed. Michael Best. 8 June 2003, http://web.uvic.ca/shakespeare/Library/SLTnoframes/drama/gorboduc.html.
A page providing brief information on *Gorboduc.*

"Selected Poetry of Thomas Sackville, Earl of Dorset (1536–1608)." *Representative Poetry Online.* 8 June 2003, http://eir.library.utoronto.ca/rpo/display/poet286.html.
The full text of Sackville's introduction to *The Mirror for Magistrates.*

Biographies and Criticism

Berlin, Normand. *Thomas Sackville.* New York: Twayne, 1974.

Cauthen, Irby B., Jr. "Thomas Sackville and Thomas Norton." Bowers, *Elizabethan Dramatists* (Dictionary of Literary Biography 62), 261–266.

Pincombe, Michael. "Thomas Sackville." Richardson, *Sixteenth-Century British Nondramatic Writers,* 1st ser. (Dictionary of Literary Biography 132), 256–262.

George Sandys, 1578–1644

Web Sites

"Ovid's Metamorphosis Englished Mythologized and Represented in Figures: Translated by George Sandys." *The Ovid Project: Metamorphosing the Metamorphoses.* Ed. Hope Greenberg. Update unknown. University of Vermont. 8 June. 2003, http://www.uvm.edu/~hag/ovid/sandys1640/sandys1640.html.
Images from the 1640 edition of Sandys's translation of Ovid's *Metamorphosis.*

Thompson, A. Hamilton. "George Sandys." *Bartleby.com.* 8 June 2003, http://www.bartleby.com/217/0303.html.
An entry on Sandys from *The Cambridge History of English and American Literature,* 1907–1921.

Biographies and Criticism

"George Sandys." *Literature Criticism from 1400 to 1800* 80: 301–390.
Excerpts of comments and criticism on Sandys from 1872–1989.

Kemp, Homer D. "George Sandys." Elliott, *American Colonial Writers, 1606–1734* (Dictionary of Literary Biography 24), 268-272.

Rubin, Deborah. "George Sandys." Hester, *Seventeenth-Century British Nondramatic Poets*: 1st ser. (Dictionary of Literary Biography 121), 235–245.

William Shakespeare, 1564–1616

Note: Individual subentries for Shakespeare's works are listed alphabetically following the standard categories below.

Web Sites

The Complete Works of William Shakespeare. Ed. Jeremy Hylton. Update unknown. Massachusetts Institute of Technology. 8 June 2003, http://the-tech.mit.edu/Shakespeare/.
The full text of Shakespeare's dramatic works.

Encyclopaedia Britannica Shakespeare and the Globe: Then and Now. 8 June 2003, http://www.britannica.com/shakespeare.
A helpful site for students. Of particular interest are the detailed sections on Shakespeare's plays and major characters. Also features sections devoted to Shakespeare's life, a history of the Globe, a study guide, and biographical information on Shakespeare's contemporaries.

"Mr. William Shakespeare and the Internet." Ed. Terry A. Gray. 7 May 2003. Palomar College. 8 June 2003, http://shakespeare.palomar.edu/.
The most exhaustive Shakespeare site on the Web and an excellent starting point for researching Shakespeare online. Particularly useful are the "Best Sites," "Life and Times," and "Criticism" sections.

"Oxford Shakespeare." *Bartleby.com.* 8 June 2003, http://www.bartleby.com/70/.
The full text of the 1914 Oxford Shakespeare. Helpful for the ability to search for words in the text, which allows users to treat the site as a concordance.

Saintsbury, George. "Shakespeare: Life and Plays" and "Shakespeare: Poems." *Bartleby.com.* 8 June 2003, http://www.bartleby.com/215/#8 and http://www.bartleby.com/215/#9.
Entries on Shakespeare from *The Cambridge History of English and American Literature,* 1907–1921. Contains numerous essays on his life and works.

The Shakespeare Birthplace Trust. 13 Dec. 2002. The Shakespeare Birthplace Trust. 8 June 2003, http://www.shakespeare.org.uk/.
The official site of the Shakespeare Birthplace Trust in Stratford-upon-Avon. Includes a FAQs (frequently asked questions) section with information on Shakespeare's life, works, and the culture of Elizabethan England. Also provides brief overviews of the plays.

The Shakespeare Classroom. Ed. J. M. Massi. 30 Sept. 2000. 8 June 2003, http://www.jetlink.net/~massij/shakes/.
Features a section addressing frequently asked questions about Shakespeare, a filmography of Shakespeare's plays, and study questions for many of his plays. This site is "permanently under construction" so check back for updates.

Shakespeare Online. Ed. Amanda Mabillard. Update unknown. 8 June 2003, http://www.shakespeare-online.com.
"Providing free and original information on Shakespeare to students, teachers, and Shakespeare enthusiasts in general," this exhaustive site features the full text of Shakespeare's plays and poems; analysis of selected plays such as *Hamlet, Romeo and Juliet, Macbeth,* and *Julius Caesar;* a biography and timeline; and a thorough collection of Shakespeare and Renaissance-related sites.

Shakespeare's Globe Research Database. Ed. Lyn Holman. June 2003. University of Reading. 8 June 2003, http://www.rdg.ac.uk/globe/.
An excellent resource for information on both the original Globe and the new Globe. Also includes the Shakespeare in Performance Research Database, which contains copies of the *Globe Research Bulletins* and Globe performance schedules.

Shakespeare's Life and Times. Ed. Michael Best. 8 June 2003, http://web.uvic.ca/shakespeare/Library/SLT/intro/introsubj.html.
A comprehensive Shakespeare site. Features ten "books" devoted to Shakespearean topics, including: "Shakespeare's life," "the stage," "the drama," and "some plays explored." A great resource for online Shakespearean research. Created by Professor Best at the University of Victoria.

Surfing with the Bard. Ed. Amy Ulen. 25 June 2003. 8 June 2003, http://www.ulen.com/shakespeare/.
"Your Shakespeare Classroom on the Internet." Click on "Plays" for links organized by play. Click on "Students" for "Shakespeare 101" a helpful introduction to Shakespeare's plays, a guide to *A Midsummer Night's Dream,* and a brief look at the life and times of Shakespeare. Also features Shakespeare-related discussion boards. Note: at the time of writing this entry, the site was in the process of being moved. If the first link is no longer working, click on "Library" at http://www.shakespearehigh.com/.

Biographies and Criticism

Andrews, John F. "William Shakespeare." Bowers, *Elizabethan Dramatists* (Dictionary of Literary Biography 62), 267–353.

Bassnett, Susan. *Shakespeare, the Elizabethan Plays.* New York: St. Martin's, 1993.

Bieman, Elizabeth. *William Shakespeare: The Romances.* Boston: Twayne, 1990.
Chapters on *Cymbeline, Pericles, The Tempest,* and *The Winter's Tale.*

Drakakis, John. *Shakespearean Tragedy.* London; New York: Longman, 1992.

Dutton, Richard. *William Shakespeare: A Literary Life.* Basingstoke: Macmillan, 1989.

Hillman, Richard. *William Shakespeare: The Problem Plays.* New York: Twayne; Toronto: Maxwell Macmillan Canada; New York: Maxwell Macmillan International, 1993.
Includes chapters on *All's Well that Ends Well, Measure for Measure,* and *Troilus and Cressida.*

Holderness, Graham, Bryan Loughrey, and Andrew Murphy. *Shakespeare: The Roman Plays.* London: Longman, 1996.

Jorgensen, Paul A. *William Shakespeare: The Tragedies.* Boston: Twayne, 1985.
Chapters on *Antony and Cleopatra, Coriolanus, Julius Caesar, Hamlet, King Lear, Macbeth, Othello, Romeo and Juliet, Timon of Athens,* and *Titus Andronicus.*

Kay, Dennis. "William Shakespeare." Richardson, *Sixteenth-Century British Nondramatic Writers,* 4th ser. (Dictionary of Literary Biography 172), 217–237.

———. *William Shakespeare: His Life and Times.* New York: Twayne; Toronto: Maxwell Macmillan Canada; New York: Maxwell Macmillan International, 1995.

Macdonald, Ronald R. *William Shakespeare: The Comedies.* New York: Twayne; Toronto: Maxwell Macmillan Canada; New York: Maxwell Macmillan International, 1992.
Discusses *As You Like It, The Comedy of Errors, Love's Labor's Lost, The Merchant of Venice, The Merry Wives of Windsor, A Midsummer Night's Dream, Much Ado about Nothing, The Taming of the Shrew, Twelfth Night,* and *The Two Gentlemen of Verona.*

McGuire, Philip C. *Shakespeare: The Jacobean Plays.* New York: St. Martin's, 1994.
Contains chapters on *Coriolanus, King Lear, Macbeth, Measure for Measure, Othello, The Tempest,* and *The Winter's Tale.*

Pearlman, E. *William Shakespeare: The History Plays.* New York: Twayne; Toronto: Maxwell Macmillan Canada; New York: Maxwell Macmillan International, 1992.
Chapters on *Henry the IV, parts 1 and* 2; *Henry V; Henry VI, parts 1, 2, and 3; Henry VIII, King John; Richard II; and Richard III.*

Shakespearean Criticism: Excerpts from the Criticism of William Shakespeare's Plays and Poetry, from the First Published Appraisals to Current Evaluations. Eds. Laurie Lanzen Harris and Mark W. Scott. Detroit: Gale, 1984–.
An exhaustive series currently comprising well over seventy volumes. As the title suggests, the series covers criticism ranging from the sixteenth to the twenty-first centuries. Volumes are arranged by entries for individual plays (varying by volume), although sometimes a particular topic will receive its own entry. Each volume contains a Cumulative Character Index and Cumulative Topic Indexes arranged by both topic and by play. The best way to use this resource is to look up a given play or topic in the indexes of the most recently published volume and then review the volumes listed therein.

Dictionaries, Encyclopedias, and Handbooks

Note: This category has been subdivided into the following categories: Dictionaries, Glossaries, and Thesauri; General Handbooks and Guides; Law; Military; Pronunciation Guides; Quotations and Coinages; Shakespeare's World; Sources; and Who's Who.

Dictionaries, Glossaries, and Thesauri

Boyce, Charles and David White. *Shakespeare A to Z: The Essential Reference to His Plays, His Poems, His Life and Times, and More.* New York: Facts on File, 1990.

Clark, Sandra. *The Penguin Shakespeare Dictionary* (Hutchinson Shakespeare Dictionary). London: Penguin, 1999.

McConnell, Louise. *Dictionary of Shakespeare.* Chicago: Fitzroy Dearborn, 2000.

Onions, C. T., and Robert D. Eagleson. *A Shakespeare Glossary.* Oxford: Clarendon, 1986.
Revised edition of Onions and Eagleson's 1911 edition published by The Clarendon Press.

Shewmaker, Eugene F. *Shakespeare's Language: A Glossary of Unfamiliar Words in Shakespeare's Plays and Poems.* New York: Facts On File, 1996.

Spevack, Marvin. *A Shakespeare Thesaurus.* Hildesheim; New York: G. Olms, 1993.

Wells, Stanley W. and James Shaw. *A Dictionary of Shakespeare.* Oxford and New York: Oxford UP, 1998.

Wells, Stanley W. *Shakespeare: An Illustrated Dictionary.* London: Kaye & Ward; New York: O UP, 1978.

West, Gilian. *A Dictionary of Shakespeare's Semantic Wordplay.* Lewiston, N.Y.: Edwin Mellen P, 1998.

Williams, Gordon. *A Glossary of Shakespeare's Sexual Language*. London; Atlantic Highlands, N.J.: Athlone P, 1997.

General Handbooks and Guides

Cahn, Victor L. *The Plays of Shakespeare: A Thematic Guide*. Westport, Conn.: Greenwood, 2001.

Campbell, Oscar James, and Edward G. Quinn. *A Shakespeare Encyclopedia* (*Reader's Encyclopedia of Shakespeare*). London: Methuen, 1966.

De Grazia, Margreta, and Stanley Wells. *The Cambridge Companion to Shakespeare*. Cambridge and New York: Cambridge UP, 2001.

Fallon, Robert Thomas. *A Theatergoer's Guide to Shakespeare*. Chicago: I. R. Dee, 2001.

Halliday, F. E. *A Shakespeare Companion, 1564–1964*. London: Duckworth, 1964.

Leggatt, Alexander. *The Cambridge Companion to Shakespearean Comedy*. Cambridge and New York: Cambridge UP, 2002.

Marsh, Nicholas. *Shakespeare, the Tragedies*. New York: St. Martin's, 1998.

McDonald, Russ. *The Bedford Companion to Shakespeare: An Introduction with Documents*. Boston: Bedford Books of St. Martin's, 1996.

Law

Sokol, B. J., and Mary Sokol. *Shakespeare's Legal Language: A Dictionary*. London and New Brunswick, N.J.: Athlone P; Somerset, N.J.: Distributed in the United States by Transaction Books, 2000.

Military

Edelman, Charles. *Shakespeare's Military Language: A Dictionary*. London and New Brunswick, N.J.: Athlone P; Somerset, N.J.: Distributed in the United States by Transaction, 2000.

Pronunciation Guides

Colaianni, Louis. *Shakespeare's Names: A New Pronouncing Dictionary*. New York: Drama, 1999.

Coye, Dale F. *Pronouncing Shakespeare's Words: A Guide from A to Zounds*. Westport, Conn.: Greenwood, 1998.

Quotations and Coinages

Armstrong, Jane. *The Arden Dictionary of Shakespeare Quotations*. Walton-on-Thames: Thomas Nelson, 1999.

Foakes, Mary, and Reginald Foakes. *The Columbia Dictionary of Quotations from Shakespeare*. New York: Columbia UP, 1998.

McQuain, Jeff, and Stanley Malless. *Coined by Shakespeare: Words and Meanings First Used by the Bard*. Springfield, Mass.: Merriam-Webster, 1998.

Miner Margaret, and Hugh Rawson. *A Dictionary of Quotations from Shakespeare: A Topical Guide to Over 3,000 Great Passages from the Plays, Sonnets, and Narrative Poems*. New York: Dutton, 1992. Reprinted by Meridian, 1996.

Shakespeare's World

Andrews, John F. *Shakespeare's World and Work: An Encyclopedia for Students*. New York: Scribner's, 2001.

Sources

Bullough, Geoffrey. *Narrative and Dramatic Sources of Shakespeare*. London: Routledge and Paul; New York, Columbia UP, 1957–1975.

Gillespie, Stuart. *Shakespeare's Books: A Dictionary of Shakespeare Sources*. London: Athlone, 2001.

Who's Who

Davis, J. Madison, and A. Daniel Frankforter. *The Shakespeare Name Dictionary*. New York: Garland, 1995.

May, Robin. *Who's Who in Shakespeare*. London: Elm Tree Books, 1972.

Palmer, Alan Warwick, and Veronica Palmer. *Who's Who in Shakespeare's England*. New York: St. Martin's, 1999.

Quennell, Peter, and Hamish Johnson. *Who's Who in Shakespeare*. New York: William Morrow, 1973.

Rowse, A. L. *Shakespeare's Characters: A Complete Guide*. London: Methuen, 1984.

Stokes, Francis Griffin. *A Dictionary of the Characters & Proper Names in the Works of Shakespeare: With Notes on the Sources and Dates of the Plays and Poems*. Gloucester, Mass.: P. Smith, 1960.
A reprint of the first edition published by G. G. Harrap, 1924.

Indexes and Concordances

Bartlett, John. *A Complete Concordance or Verbal Index to Words, Phrases and Passages in the Dramatic Works of Shakespeare, with a Supplementary Concordance to the Poems*. London: Macmillan; New York: St. Martin's, 1953.
Based on the Globe edition of Shakespeare (1875 and 1891).

Furness, Horace Howard. *A Concordance to Shakespeare's Poems: An Index to Every Word Therein Contained*. New York: AMS P, 1972.

Spevack, Marvin. *A Complete and Systematic concordance to the Works of Shakespeare.* Hildesheim, Germany: Olms, 1968–.
    Based on G. Blackmore Evans's *The Riverside Shakespeare* (Boston: Houghton Mifflin, 1974).

Journals

Selected Papers from the West Virginia Shakespeare and Renaissance Association. Morgantown: West Virginia University Foundation, 1976–.

Shakespeare Bulletin. Norwood, N.J.: New York Shakespeare Society, 1983–.

The Shakespearean International Yearbook. Aldershot, England, and Brookfield, Vt.: Ashgate, 1999–.

Shakespeare on Film Newsletter. Burlington, Vt.: Offset House, 1976–1992.

Shakespeare Quarterly. Washington, D.C.: Folger Shakespeare Library, 1950–.

Shakespeare Studies. Tokyo: Shakespeare Society of Japan, 1962–.

Shakespeare Survey. Cambridge and New York: Cambridge UP, 1948–.

Shakespeare Yearbook. Lewiston, N.Y.: Edwin Mellen P, 1990–.

The Upstart Crow. Martin, Tenn.: Upstart Crow, 1978–.

Bibliographies

Bergeron, David Moore, and Geraldo U. de Sousa. *Shakespeare: A Study and Research Guide.* Lawrence: UP Kansas, 1995.

Champion, Larry S. *The Essential Shakespeare: An Annotated Bibliography of Major Modern Studies.* New York: G. K. Hall; Toronto: Maxwell Macmillan Canada; New York: Maxwell Macmillan International, 1993.

Elton, William R., and Giselle Schlesinger. *Shakespeare's World: Renaissance Intellectual Contexts: A Selective, Annotated Guide, 1966–1971.* New York: Garland, 1979.

Guttman, Selma. *The Foreign Sources of Shakespeare's Works; An Annotated Bibliography of the Commentary Written on This Subject Between 1904 and 1940, Together with Lists of Certain Translations Available to Shakespeare.* New York, King's Crown P, 1947. Reprinted by Octagon Books, 1968.

Hayashi, Tetsumaro. *Shakespeare's Sonnets: A Record of 20th-century Criticism.* Metuchen, N.J.: Scarecrow, 1972.

Hotaling, Edward R., *Shakespeare and the Musical Stage: A Guide to Sources, Studies, and First Performances.* Boston: G. K. Hall, 1990.

Howard-Hill, T. H. *Shakespearian Bibliography and Textual Criticism: A Bibliography.* Signal Mountain, Tenn.: Summertown, 2000.

Jacobs, Henry E., and Claudia D. Johnson. *An Annotated Bibliography of Shakespearean Burlesques, Parodies, and Travesties.* New York: Garland, 1976.

Kolin, Philip C. *Shakespeare and Feminist Criticism: An Annotated Bibliography and Commentary.* New York: Garland, 1991.

Kujoory, Parvin. *Shakespeare and Minorities: An Annotated Bibliography, 1970–2000.* Lanham, Md.: Scarecrow P, 2001.

McRoberts, J. Paul. *Shakespeare and the Medieval Tradition: An Annotated Bibliography.* New York, NY: Garland, 1985.

Metz, G. Harold. *Four Plays Ascribed to Shakespeare: The Reign of King Edward III, Sir Thomas More, The History of Cardenio, The Two Noble Kinsmen: An Annotated Bibliography.* New York: Garland, 1982.

O'Dell, Leslie. *Shakespearean Scholarship: A Guide for Actors and Students.* Westport, Conn.: Greenwood P, 2002.

Richmond, Hugh Macrae. *Shakespeare and the Renaissance stage to 1616: Shakespearean Stage History 1616 to 1998: An Annotated Bibliography of Shakespeare Studies, 1576–1998.* Asheville, N.C.: Pegasus P, 1999.

Sajdak, Bruce T. *Shakespeare Index: An Annotated Bibliography of Critical Articles on the Plays, 1959–1983.* Millwood, N.Y.: Kraus International, 1992.

Thompson, Ann, Thomas L. Berger, et al.*Which Shakespeare?: A User's Guide to Editions.* Milton Keynes, England and Philadelphia: Open UP, 1992.

Walker, Lewis. *Shakespeare and the Classical Tradition: An Annotated Bibliography, 1961–1991.* New York: Routledge, 2002.

Wells, Stanley. *Shakespeare, a Bibliographical Guide.* Oxford, England: Clarendon P; New York: Oxford UP, 1990.

Woodbridge, Linda. *Shakespeare, a Selective Bibliography of Modern Criticism.* West Cornwall, Conn.: Locust Hill P, 1988.

Shakespeare's Works

All's Well That Ends Well

Web Sites

"Study Questions for Shakespeare's *All's Well That Ends Well.*" *The Shakespeare Classroom.* 26 June 2003, http://www.jetlink.net/~massij/wssq/allswell.htm. Study questions for *All's Well that Ends Well.*

Biographies and Criticism

Zitner, Sheldon P. *All's Well That Ends Well.* New York: Harvester Wheatsheaf, 1989.

Antony and Cleopatra

"Antony and Cleopatra." 8 June 2003,http://www.cas.buffalo.edu/classes/eng/willbern/
Shakespeare/plays/Antony/antony.htm.
    Features study questions, lecture notes, and links to *Antony and Cleopatra*–related
sites.

"The Triumph of the Lions? An Introduction to *Antony and Cleopatra."* 8 Jun 2003,
http://www.mala.bc.ca/~johnstoi/eng366/lectures/antonycleopatra.htm.
    A comprehensive introduction to *Antony and Cleopatra.*

Dictionaries, Encyclopedias, and Handbooks

Hall, Joan Lord. *"Antony and Cleopatra": A Guide to the Play.* Westport, Conn.:
Greenwood, 2002.

As You Like It

Web Sites

"As You Like It." 8 June 2003, http://www.cas.buffalo.edu/classes/eng/willbern/Shakespeare/
plays/AYLI/AYLI.htm.
    Features study questions, lecture notes, and links to *As You Like It*–related sites.

"Study Questions for Shakespeare's *As You Like It." The Shakespeare Classroom.* 26
June 2003, http://www.jetlink.net/~massij/wssq/ayli.html.
    Study questions for *As You Like It.*

"Variations on a Theme of Love: An Introduction to *As You Like It."* 8 June 2003,
http://www.mala.bc.ca/~johnstoi/eng366/lectures/Ayl.htm.
    A detailed introduction to *As You Like It.*

Biographies and Criticism

Tomarken, Edward. *"As You Like It" from 1600 to the Present: Critical Essays.* New
York: Garland, 1997.

Ward, John Powell. *As You Like It.* New York: Twayne, 1992.

Bibliographies

Halio, Jay L., and Barbara C. Millard. *"As You like It": An Annotated Bibliography,
1940–1980.* New York: Garland, 1985.

The Comedy of Errors

Web Sites

"The Comedy of Errors." 8 June 2003, http://www.cas.buffalo.edu/classes/eng/
willbern/Shakespeare/plays/Errors/errors.htm.
    Features study questions, lecture notes, and links to *The Comedy of Errors*–related
sites.

"Study Questions for Shakespeare's *The Comedy of Errors.*" *The Shakespeare Classroom.* 26 June 2003, http://www.jetlink.net/~massij/wssq/comedy.htm.
Study questions for *The Comedy of Errors.*

Biographies and Criticism

Miola, Robert S. *"The Comedy of Errors": Critical Essays.* New York: Garland, 1997.

Coriolanus

Web Sites

"Study Questions for Shakespeare's *Coriolanus.*" *The Shakespeare Classroom.* 26 June 2003, http://www.jetlink.net/~massij/wssq/coriol.html.
Study questions for *Coriolanus.*

Biographies and Criticism

Poole, Adrian. *Coriolanus.* Boston: Twayne, 1988.

Wheeler, David. *"Coriolanus": Critical Essays.* New York: Garland, 1995.

Bibliographies

Leggatt, Alexander, and Lois Norem. *"Coriolanus": An Annotated Bibliography.* New York: Garland, 1989.

Cymbeline

Web Sites

"*Cymbeline.*" *Encyclopaedia Britannica Presents Shakespeare and the Globe: Then and Now.* 30 June 2003, http://www.britannica.com/shakespeare/micro/731/46.html.
A brief overview of the play with hyperlinks to character descriptions.

Bibliographies

Jacobs, Henry E. *Cymbeline.* New York: Garland, 1982.

Hamlet

Web Sites

"*Hamlet.*" 8 June 2003, http://www.cas.buffalo.edu/classes/eng/willbern/Shakespeare/plays/Hamlet/hamlet.htm.
Features study questions, lecture notes, and links to *Hamlet*-related sites.

"Introductory Lecture on Shakespeare's *Hamlet.*" 8 June 2003, http://www.mala. bc.ca/~johnstoi/eng366/lectures/hamlet.htm.
A comprehensive introduction to *Hamlet.*

"Study Questions for Shakespeare's *Hamlet.*" *The Shakespeare Classroom.* 26 June 2003, http://www.jetlink.net/~massij/wssq/hamlet.html.
Study questions for *Hamlet.*

"*The Tragedy of Hamlet, Prince of Denmark.*" 8 June 2003, http://www.facweb. stvincent.edu/Academics/English/el315/hamlet/.
A slideshow lecture focusing on the background of *Hamlet.* Includes notes on the play's sources and information on Senecan tragedy and English revenge tragedy.

Biographies and Criticism

Watts, Cedric Thomas. *Hamlet.* Boston: Twayne, 1988.

Dictionaries, Encyclopedias, and Handbooks

MacCary, W. Thomas. "*Hamlet*": *A Guide to the Play.* Westport, Conn.: Greenwood, 1998.

Journals

Hamlet Studies. New Delhi: Vikas, 1979–.

Bibliographies

Dietrich, Julia. "*Hamlet*" *in the 1960s: An Annotated Bibliography.* New York: Garland, 1992.

Mooney, Michael E. "*Hamlet*": *An Annotated Bibliography of Shakespeare Studies, 1604–1998.* Asheville, N.C.: Pegasus P, 1999.

Raven, Anton Adolph. *A* "*Hamlet*" *Bibliography and Reference Guide, 1877–1935.* New York: Russell & Russell, 1966.

Robinson, Randal F. "*Hamlet*" *in the 1950's: An Annotated Bibliography.* New York: Garland, 1984.

Henry IV, Parts 1 and 2

Web Sites

"The Foxes, the Lion, and the Fat Knight: Introduction to *Henry IV, Part 1.*" 8 June 2003, http://www.mala.bc.ca/~johnstoi/eng366/lectures/henry4.htm.
A comprehensive introduction to *Henry IV, Part 1.*

"*Henry IV Part 1.*" 8 June 2003, http://www.cas.buffalo.edu/classes/eng/willbern/ Shakespeare/plays/Henry4/henry4.htm.
Features study questions, lecture notes, and links to *Henry IV, Part 1*–related sites.

"Study Questions for Shakespeare's *Henry IV, Part One.*" *The Shakespeare Classroom.*
26 June 2003, http://www.jetlink.net/~massij/wssq/1h4.html.
Study questions for *Henry IV, Part 1.*

"Study Questions for Shakespeare's *Henry IV, Part Two.*" *The Shakespeare Classroom.*
26 June 2003, http://www.jetlink.net/~massij/wssq/2h4.html.
Study questions for *Henry IV, Part 2.*

Biographies and Criticism

Bevington, David. *"Henry the Fourth," parts I and II: Critical Essays.* New York: Garland, 1986.

Bibliographies

Candido, Joseph. *"Richard II," "Henry IV," parts I and II, and "Henry V": An Annotated Bibliography of Shakespeare Studies, 1777–1997.* Asheville, NC: Pegasus P, 1998.

Gira, Catherine, and Adele Seeff. *"Henry IV", Parts 1 and 2: An Annotated Bibliography.* New York: Garland, 1994.

Knowles, Ronald. *"Henry IV", Parts I & II.* Basingstoke, England: Macmillan, 1992.

Henry V

Web Sites

"Henry V: A Historie by William Shakespeare." Ed. Nola Smith and Bob Nelson. 8 June 2003, http://www.nauvoo.byu.edu/TheArts/Theater/studypackets/Lesson14/main.html.
Features information on the historical, political, and theatrical backgrounds of the play, as well as brief act summaries and character overviews.

"The Ironies of Success in Politics: An Introduction to Shakespeare's *Henry V.*" 8 June 2003, http://www.mala.bc.ca/~johnstoi/eng366/lectures/henry5.htm.
A comprehensive introduction to *Henry V.*

Biographies and Criticism

Brennan, Anthony. *Henry V.* New York: Twayne, 1992.

Dictionaries, Encyclopedias, and Handbooks

Hall, Joan Lord. *"Henry V": A Guide to the Play.* Westport, Conn.: Greenwood, 1997.

Bibliographies

Candido, Joseph, and Charles R. Forker. *"Henry V": An Annotated Bibliography.* New York: Garland, 1983.

Candido, Joseph. *"Richard II", "Henry IV", parts I and II, and "Henry V": An Annotated Bibliography of Shakespeare Studies, 1777–1997.* Asheville, N.C.: Pegasus P, 1998.

Henry VI, Parts 1, 2, and 3

Web Sites

"Henry VI Parts 1, 2, and 3." Encyclopaedia Britannica Presents Shakespeare and the Globe: Then and Now. 30 June 2003, http://www.britannica.com/shakespeare/micro/729/59.html, http://www.britannica.com/shakespeare/micro/729/60.html, and http://www.britannica.com/shakespeare/micro/729/62.html.
Overview of the plays with hyperlinks to character descriptions.

Biographies and Criticism

Pendleton, Thomas A. *"Henry VI": Critical Essays.* New York: Routledge, 2001.

Bibliographies

Hinchcliffe, Judith. *"King Henry VI", Parts 1, 2, and 3: An Annotated Bibliography.* New York: Garland, 1984.

Henry VIII (All Is True)

Web Sites

"Henry VIII." Encyclopaedia Britannica Presents Shakespeare and the Globe: Then and Now. 30 June 2003, http://www.britannica.com/shakespeare/micro/729/93.html.
An overview of the play with hyperlinks to character descriptions.

Biographies and Criticism

Shirley, Frances A. *"King John" and "Henry VIII": Critical Essays.* New York: Garland, 1988.

Bibliographies

Micheli, Linda McJ. *"Henry VIII": An Annotated Bibliography.* New York: Garland, 1988.

Julius Caesar

Web Sites

"Julius Caesar." 8 June 2003, http://www.cas.buffalo.edu/classes/eng/willbern/Shakespeare/plays/Caesar/caesar.htm.
Features study questions, lecture notes, and links to *Julius Caesar*–related sites.

"Study Questions for Shakespeare's *Julius Caesar.*" *The Shakespeare Classroom.* 26 June 2003, http://www.jetlink.net/~massij/wssq/caesar.html.
Study questions for *Julius Caesar.*

Biographies and Criticism

Thomas, Vivian. *Julius Caesar.* New York: Twayne, 1992.

Dictionaries, Encyclopedias, and Handbooks

McMurtry, Jo. *"Julius Caesar": A Guide to the Play.* Westport, Conn.: Greenwood, 1998.

King John

Web Sites

"King John." Encyclopaedia Britannica Presents Shakespeare and the Globe: Then and Now. 30 June 2003, http://www.britannica.com/shakespeare/micro/730/41.html.
An overview of *King John* with hyperlinks to character descriptions.

Biographies and Criticism

Shirley, Frances A. *"King John" and "Henry VIII": Critical Essays.* New York: Garland, 1988.

Bibliographies

Curren-Aquino, Deborah T. *"King John": An Annotated Bibliography.* New York: Garland, 1994

King Lear

Web Sites

"King Lear." 8 June 2003, http://www.cas.buffalo.edu/classes/eng/willbern/Shakespeare/plays/Lear/lear.htm.
Features study questions, lecture notes, and links to *King Lear*–related sites.

"Shakespeare in Context: *King Lear.*" *The English Renaissance in Context* (ERIC). 8 June 2003, http://oldsite.library.upenn.edu/etext/collections/furness/eric/teach/index.htm.
A multimedia tutorial on *King Lear.* The slideshow may run fast on your browser, so be prepared to hit the pause button.

"Speak What We Feel: An Introduction to *King Lear.*" 8 June 2003, http://www.mala.bc.ca/~johnstoi/eng366/lectures/lear.htm.
A comprehensive introduction to *King Lear.*

"Study Questions for Shakespeare's *King Lear.*" *The Shakespeare Classroom.* 26 June 2003, http://www.jetlink.net/~massij/wssq/lear.html.
Study questions for *King Lear.*

Biographies and Criticism

Leggatt, Alexander. *King Lear*. Boston: Twayne, 1988.

Muir, Kenneth. *"King Lear": Critical Essays*. New York: Garland, 1984.

Dictionaries, Encyclopedias, and Handbooks

Halio, Jay L. *"King Lear": A Guide to the Play*. Westport, Conn.: Greenwood, 2001.

Bibliographies

Bushnell, Rebecca W. *"King Lear" and "Macbeth", 1674–1995: An Annotated Bibliography of Shakespeare Studies*. Asheville, N.C. : Pegasus, University of North Carolina, 1996.

Champion, Larry S. *"King Lear", an Annotated Bibliography*. New York: Garland, 1980.

Love's Labour's Lost

Web Sites

"Love's Labour's Lost: Table of Contents." 8 June 2003, http://www.engl.uvic.ca/Faculty/MBHomePage/ISShakespeare/LLLCourse/LLLtoc.html.
An academic site devoted to *Love's Labour's Lost*. Includes a self-test, study questions, background reading, and commentary on the play.

"Study Questions for Shakespeare's *Love's Labour's Lost.*" The Shakespeare Classroom. 26 June 2003, http://www.jetlink.net/~massij/wssq/lll.htm.
Study questions for *Love's Labour's Lost*.

Biographies and Criticism

Londré, Felicia Hardison. *"Love's Labour's Lost": Critical Essays*. New York: Garland, 1997.

Dictionaries, Encyclopedias, and Handbooks

Pendergast, John S. *"Love's Labour's Lost": A Guide to the Play*. Westport, Conn.: Greenwood, 2002.

Bibliographies

Huffman, Clifford Chalmers. *"Love's Labor's Lost," "A Midsummer Night's Dream," and "The Merchant of Venice": An Annotated Bibliography of Shakespeare Studies, 1888–1994*. Binghamton, N.Y.: Medieval and Renaissance Texts and Studies, 1995.

Harvey, Nancy Lenz, and Anna Kirwan Carey. *"Love's Labor's Lost": An Annotated Bibliography*. New York: Garland, 1984.

Macbeth

Web Sites

"Macbeth." 8 June 2003, http://www.cas.buffalo.edu/classes/eng/willbern/Shakespeare/plays/
Macbeth/macbeth.htm.
Features study questions, lecture notes, and links to *Macbeth*-related sites.

"Study Questions for Shakespeare's *Macbeth." The Shakespeare Classroom.* 26 June
2003, http://www.jetlink.net/~massij/wssq/macbeth.html.
Study questions for *Macbeth.*

"William Shakespeare's *Macbeth."* Ed. Bob Nelson. 8 June 2003, http://www.
nauvoo.byu.edu/TheArts/Theater/studypackets/lesson09/main.html.
Features the essays "Monstrous Excess: Ideas on Gender in Shakespeare's
Macbeth," "Staging Shakespeare's *Macbeth,"* and "Shakespeare's *Macbeth:* A Study
of the Dark Side and Its Limits." Also includes a chronology of Shakespeare's plays and
a chronology of Shakespeare's life.

Biographies and Criticism

Long, Michael. *Macbeth.* Boston: Twayne, 1989.

Dictionaries, Encyclopedias, and Handbooks

Bloom, Harold. *William Shakespeare's "Macbeth."* New York: Chelsea House, 1996.

Coursen, Herbert R. *"Macbeth": A Guide to the Play.* Westport, Conn.: Greenwood,
1997.

Bibliographies

Bushnell, Rebecca W. *"King Lear" and "Macbeth," 1674–1995: An Annotated Bibliography of Shakespeare Studies.* Asheville, N.C.: Pegasus, University of North
Carolina, 1996.

Wheeler, Thomas. *"Macbeth," an Annotated Bibliography.* New York: Garland, 1990.

Measure for Measure

Web Sites

"Measure for Measure." 8 June 2003, http://www.cas.buffalo.edu/classes/eng/willbern/
Shakespeare/plays/Measure/measure.htm.
Features study questions, lecture notes, and links to *Measure for Measure*–related
sites.

"Measure for Measure." The Interactive Shakespeare Project at Holy Cross. Update
unknown. College of the Holy Cross. 8 June 2003, http://www.holycross.edu/departments/
theatre/projects/isp/measure/mainmenu.html.

A ground-breaking site for the study and teaching of Shakespeare's *Measure for Measure*. The full text of each scene is enhanced with annotations, study prompts, and movie clips. Includes classroom exercises, essays, and a teacher's guide.

Biographies and Criticism

Hawkins, Harriett. *Measure for Measure*. Boston: Twayne, 1987.

The Merchant of Venice

Web Sites

"*The Merchant of Venice*." 8 June 2003, http://www.cas.buffalo.edu/classes/eng/ willbern/Shakespeare/plays/Merchant/merch.htm.
Features study questions, lecture notes, and links to *The Merchant of Venice*–related sites.

"*The Merchant of Venice*." 8 June 2003, http://facweb.stvincent.edu/Academics/English/ el315/merchant/index.htm.
A slideshow lecture on *The Merchant of Venice*.

"Shakespeare in Context: *The Merchant of Venice*." *The English Renaissance in Context* (ERIC). 8 June 2003, http://oldsite.library.upenn.edu/etext/collections/furness/ eric/teach/index.htm.
A multimedia tutorial on *The Merchant of Venice*. The slideshow may run fast on your browser so be prepared to hit the pause button.

Stirling, Grant. "Shakespeare and Anti-Semitism: The Question of Shylock." February 1997. 8 June 2003, http://www.geocities.com/Athens/Acropolis/7221.
A Web site exploring anti-Semitism in Elizabethan England and in Shakespeare's *Merchant of Venice*. Includes sections on the "History of Jews in England," a "Stage History of Shylock," and a "Textual Analysis of *The Merchant of Venice*." Also provides a brief bibliography for further reading. Created by Grant Stirling, a former lecturer at York University in Toronto, Canada.

Biographies and Criticism

"*The Merchant of Venice*": *New Critical Essays*. Eds. John W. Mahon and Ellen Macleod Mahon. New York: Routledge, 2002

Smith, Rob. *Shakespeare, "The Merchant of Venice."* Cambridge and New York: Cambridge UP, 2002.

Bibliographies

Huffman, Clifford Chalmers. "*Love's Labor's Lost*," "*A Midsummer Night's Dream*," and "*The Merchant of Venice*": *An Annotated Bibliography of Shakespeare Studies, 1888–1994*. Binghamton, N.Y.: Medieval & Renaissance Texts & Studies, 1995.

Wheeler, Thomas. "*The Merchant of Venice*": *An Annotated Bibliography*. New York: Garland, 1985.

The Merry Wives of Windsor

Web Sites

"Shakespeare's *The Merry Wives of Windsor.*" Ed. Bob Nelson. 8 June 2003, http://www.nauvoo.byu.edu/TheArts/Theater/studypackets/lesson07/main.html.
Includes notes on *The Merry Wives of Windsor,* a chronology of Shakespeare's plays, a chronology of Shakespeare's life, and an essay entitled "Gender Matters in *The Merry Wives of Windsor.*"

Biographies and Criticism

White, R. S. *The Merry Wives of Windsor.* London: Harvester Wheatsheaf, 1991.

A Midsummer Night's Dream

Web Sites

"EL 315 Shakespeare's Comedies and Tragedies." 8 June 2003, http://facweb.stvincent.edu/Academics/English/el315/mnd/index.htm.
A slideshow introduction to *A Midsummer Night's Dream.*

"*A Midsummer Night's Dream.*" Ed. Nola Smith and Bob Nelson. 8 June 2003, http://www.nauvoo.byu.edu/TheArts/Theater/studypackets/Lesson22/main.htm.
Features a brief plot summary by act, an overview of the characters, and essays on the play's structure and sources.

"*A Midsummer Night's Dream.*" 8 June 2003, http://www.cas.buffalo.edu/classes/eng/willbern/Shakespeare/plays/MND/MND.htm.
Features study questions, lecture notes, and links to *A Midsummer Night's Dream*–related sites.

"Reading Notes for Shakespeare's *A Midsummer Night's Dream.*" Ed. Steven Marx. Update unknown. Cal Poly University, San Luis Obispo. 8 June 2003, http://cla.calpoly.edu/~smarx/Shakespeare/Shlectures/MNDnotes.html.
Reading notes and study prompts for *A Midsummer Night's Dream.*

"Study Questions for Shakespeare's *A Midsummer Night's Dream.*" *The Shakespeare Classroom.* 26 June 2003, http://www.jetlink.net/~massij/wssq/mnd.html.
Study questions for *A Midsummer Night's Dream.*

Biographies and Criticism

Calderwood, James L. *A Midsummer Night's Dream.* New York: Twayne, 1992.

Kehler, Dorothea. "*A Midsummer Night's Dream*": *Critical Essays.* New York: Garland, 1998.

Bibliographies

Carroll, D. Allen, and Gary Jay Williams. *"A Midsummer Night's Dream": An Annotated Bibliography*. New York: Garland, 1986.

Huffman, Clifford Chalmers. *"Love's Labor's Lost," "A Midsummer Night's Dream," and "The Merchant of Venice": An Annotated Bibliography of Shakespeare Studies, 1888–1994*. Binghamton, N.Y.: Medieval and Renaissance Texts and Studies, 1995.

Much Ado about Nothing

Web Sites

"Study Questions for Shakespeare's *Much Ado about Nothing*." *The Shakespeare Classroom*. 26 June 2003, http://www.jetlink.net/~massij/wssq/muchado.html. Study questions for *Much Ado about Nothing*.

Biographies and Criticism

Clamp, Michael. *Shakespeare: "Much Ado About Nothing."* Cambridge and New York: Cambridge UP, 2002.

Othello

Web Sites

"*Othello*." 8 June 2003, http://www.cas.buffalo.edu/classes/eng/willbern/Shakespeare/plays/Othello/othello.htm.
Features study questions, lecture notes, and links to *Othello*-related sites.

"Shakespeare, *Othello*: Study Questions." 8 June 2003, http://smith.hanover.edu/sqothello.html.
Study questions for *Othello*.

Biographies and Criticism

Kolin, Philip C. *"Othello": New Critical Essays*. New York: Routledge, 2002.

Snyder, Susan. *"Othello": Critical Essays*. New York: Garland, 1988.

Dictionaries, Encyclopedias, and Handbooks

Hall, Joan Lord. *"Othello": A Guide to the Play*. Westport, Conn.: Greenwood, 1999.

Bibliographies

Mikesell, Margaret Lael, and Virginia Mason Vaughan. *"Othello," an Annotated Bibliography*. New York: Garland, 1990.

Smith, John Hazel. *Shakespeare's "Othello": A Bibliography.* New York: AMS P, 1988.

Pericles

Web Sites

"Pericles." Encyclopaedia Britannica Presents Shakespeare and the Globe: Then and Now. 30 June 2003, http://www.britannica.com/shakespeare/micro/730/97.html. An overview of the play with hyperlinks to character descriptions.

Biographies and Criticism

Skeele, David. *"Pericles": Critical Essays.* New York: Garland, 2000.

Bibliographies

Michael, Nancy C. *"Pericles," an Annotated Bibliography.* New York: Garland, 1987.

Richard II

Web Sites

"Richard II." 8 June 2003, http://www.cas.buffalo.edu/classes/eng/willbern/Shakespeare/plays/Richard2/rich2.htm.
Features study questions, lecture notes, and links to *Richard II*–related sites.

"Richard II: Table of Contents." 8 June 2003, http://www.engl.uvic.ca/Faculty/MBHomePage/ISShakespeare/R2Course/R2toc.html.
An academic site devoted to *Richard II.* Includes a self-test, study questions, and commentary on the play.

Biographies and Criticism

Newlin, Jeanne F. *"Richard II": Critical Essays.* New York: Garland, 1984.

Bibliographies

Candido, Joseph. *"Richard II," "Henry IV," Parts I and II, and "Henry V": An Annotated Bibliography of Shakespeare Studies, 1777–1997.* Asheville, N.C.: Pegasus, 1998.

Roberts, Josephine A. *"Richard II": An Annotated Bibliography.* New York: Garland, 1988.

Richard III

Web Sites

"Lecture on Shakespeare's Transformation of Medieval Tragedy and an Introduction to *Richard III.*" 8 June 2003, http://www.mala.bc.ca/~johnstoi/eng366/lectures/lecture1b.htm.
A comprehensive introduction to *Richard III.*

"*Richard III.*" 8 June 2003, http://www.cas.buffalo.edu/classes/eng/willbern/Shakespeare/plays/Richard3/rich3.htm.
Features study questions, lecture notes, and links to *Richard III*–related sites.

"Shakespeare in Context: *Richard III.*" *The English Renaissance in Context* (ERIC). 8 June 2003, http://oldsite.library.upenn.edu/etext/collections/furness/eric/teach/index.htm.
A multimedia tutorial on *Richard III.* The slideshow may run fast on your browser so be prepared to hit the pause button.

"Study Questions for William Shakespeare's *Richard III* (ca. 1592–93)." *The Shakespeare Classroom.* 26 June 2003, http://www.jetlink.net/~massij/wssq/r3.html.
Study questions for *Richard III.*

Biographies and Criticism

Richmond, Hugh Macrae. *Critical Essays on Shakespeare's "Richard III."* New York: G. K. Hall, 1999.

Bibliographies

Moore, James A. *"Richard III": An Annotated Bibliography.* New York: Garland, 1986.

Romeo and Juliet

Web Sites

"*Romeo and Juliet.*" 8 June 2003, http://www.cas.buffalo.edu/classes/eng/willbern/Shakespeare/plays/Romeo/romeo.htm.
Features study questions, lecture notes, and links to *Romeo and Juliet*–related sites.

"*Romeo and Juliet.*" 8 June 2003, http://www.engl.uvic.ca/Faculty/MBHomePage/ISShakespeare/RJCourse/RJtoc.html.
An academic site devoted to *Romeo and Juliet.* Includes a self-test, study questions, and commentary on the play.

"Shakespeare in Context: *Romeo and Juliet.*" *The English Renaissance in Context* (ERIC). June 2003, http://oldsite.library.upenn.edu/etext/collections/furness/eric/teach/index.htm.
A multimedia tutorial on *Romeo and Juliet.* The slideshow may run fast on your browser so be prepared to hit the pause button.

"Study Questions for Shakespeare's *Romeo and Juliet.*" *The Shakespeare Classroom.* 26 June 2003, http://www.jetlink.net/~massij/wssq/rj.htm.
Study questions for *Romeo and Juliet.*

"William Shakespeare's *Romeo and Juliet.*" Ed. Nola Smith and Bob Nelson. 8 June 2003, http://www.nauvoo.byu.edu/TheArts/Theater/studypackets/lesson15/main.htm.
Features a study guide, and introduction to biographical and historic background, a plot synopsis, and character overviews.

Biographies and Criticism

Watts, Cedric Thomas. *Romeo and Juliet.* Boston: Twayne, 1991.

Dictionaries, Encyclopedias, and Handbooks

Hager, Alan. *Understanding "Romeo and Juliet": A Student Casebook to Issues, Sources, and Historical Documents.* Westport, Conn.: Greenwood, 1999.

Halio, Jay L. *"Romeo and Juliet": A Guide to the Play.* Westport, Conn.: Greenwood, 1998.

The Sonnets and Poems

Web Sites

"Shakespeare's Sonnets: Study Questions." 8 June 2003, http://smith.hanover.edu/sqsonnets.html.
Study questions for Shakespeare's sonnets. Keyed to the *Longman Anthology of British Literature,* 2d ed.

"The Sonnets: Table of Contents." 8 June 2003, http://www.engl.uvic.ca/Faculty/MBHomePage/ISShakespeare/SonCourse/Sontoc.html.
An academic site devoted to Shakespeare's sonnets. Includes a self-test, study plan, and commentary on the play.

Biographies and Criticism

Kay, Dennis. *William Shakespeare: Sonnets and Poems.* New York: Twayne; London: Prentice Hall International, 1998.

Kolin, Philip C. *"Venus and Adonis": Critical Essays.* New York: Garland, 1997.

Schiffer, James. *Shakespeare's Sonnets: Critical Essays.* New York: Garland, 1999.

The Taming of the Shrew

Web Sites

"Study Questions for Shakespeare's *The Taming of the Shrew.*" *The Shakespeare Classroom.* 26 June 2003, http://www.jetlink.net/~massij/wssq/shrew.html.
Study questions for *The Taming of the Shrew.*

Biographies and Criticism

Aspinall, Dana E. *"The Taming of the Shrew": Critical Essays.* New York: Routledge, 2002.

Bibliographies

Harvey, Nancy Lenz. *"The Taming of the Shrew": An Annotated Bibliography.* New York: Garland, 1994.

The Tempest

Web Sites

"The Tempest." 8 June 2003, http://www.cas.buffalo.edu/classes/eng/willbern/Shakespeare/plays/Tempest/tempest.htm.
Features study questions, lecture notes, and links to sites relating to *The Tempest*.

"You Can Go Home Again, Can't You? An Introduction to *The Tempest."* 8 June 2003, http://www.mala.bc.ca/~johnstoi/eng366/lectures/tempest.htm.
A comprehensive introduction to *The Tempest*.

Biographies and Criticism

Murphy, Patrick M. *The Tempest: Critical Essays.* New York: Routledge, 2001.

Dictionaries, Encyclopedias, and Handbooks

Coursen, Herbert R. *The Tempest: A Guide to the Play.* Westport, Conn.: Greenwood, 2000.

Timon of Athens

Web Sites

"Timon of Athens." Encyclopaedia Britannica Presents Shakespeare and the Globe: Then and Now. 30 June 2003, http://www.britannica.com/shakespeare/micro/731/76.html.
An overview of the play with hyperlinks to character descriptions.

Biographies and Criticism

Nuttall, A. D. *Timon of Athens.* Boston: Twayne, 1989.

Bibliographies

Elton, William R., and E. A. Rauchut. *A Selective Annotated Bibliography of Shakespeare's "Timon of Athens."* Lewiston, N.Y.: E. Mellen P, 1991.

Ruszkiewicz, John J. *"Timon of Athens": An Annotated Bibliography.* New York: Garland, 1986.

Titus Andronicus

Web Sites

"Study Questions for Shakespeare's *Titus Andronicus.*" *The Shakespeare Classroom.*
26 June 2003, http://www.jetlink.net/~massij/wssq/titus.html.
Study questions for *Titus Andronicus.*

"*Titus Andronicus.*" 8 June 2003, http://www.cas.buffalo.edu/classes/eng/willbern/
Shakespeare/plays/Titus/titus.htm.
Features study questions, lecture notes, and links to *Titus Andronicus*–related sites.

Biographies and Criticism

Kolin, Philip C. "*Titus Andronicus*": *Critical Essays.* New York: Garland, 1995.

Troilus and Cressida

Web Sites

"Study Guide: Shakespeare's *Troilus and Cressida.*" Ed. Diane Thompson. 2 Jan. 2003.
Northern Virginia Community College. 29 June 2003, http://novaonline.nv.cc.
va.us/eli/Troy/shakespeareguide.htm.
A comprehensive study guide for Shakespeare's *Troilus and Cressida.*

Biographies and Criticism

Adamson, Jane. *Troilus and Cressida.* Boston: Twayne, 1987.

Twelfth Night

Web Sites

"The Ironies of Happy Endings: An Introduction to *Twelfth Night.*" 8 June 2003,
http://www.mala.bc.ca/~johnstoi/eng366/lectures/twelfthnight.htm.
A comprehensive introduction to *Twelfth Night.*

"Shakespeare, *Twelfth Night:* Study Questions." 8 June 2003, http://smith.hanover.
edu/sqtn.html.
Study questions for *Twelfth Night.*

"*Twelfth Night.*" 8 June 2003, http://www.cas.buffalo.edu/classes/eng/willbern/Shakespeare/
plays/12Night/12N.htm.
Features study questions, lecture notes, and links to *Twelfth Night*–related sites.

Biographies and Criticism

Wells, Stanley. "*Twelfth Night*": *Critical Essays.* New York: Garland, 1986.

Bibliographies

McAvoy, William C. *"Twelfth Night, or, What You Will": A Bibliography to Supplement the New Variorum Edition of 1901*. New York: Modern Language Association of America, 1984.

The Two Gentlemen of Verona

Web Sites

"The Two Gentlemen of Verona." Encyclopaedia Britannica Presents Shakespeare and the Globe: Then and Now. 30 June 2003, http://www.britannica.com/shakespeare/micro/730/75.html.
An overview of the play with hyperlinks to character descriptions.

Biographies and Criticism

Schlueter, June. *"Two Gentlemen of Verona": Critical Essays*. New York: Garland, 1996.

Bibliographies

Pearson, D'Orsay W. *"Two Gentlemen of Verona": An Annotated Bibliography*. New York: Garland, 1988.

The Two Noble Kinsmen

Web Sites

"The Two Noble Kinsmen." Encyclopaedia Britannica Presents Shakespeare and the Globe: Then and Now. 30 June 2003, http://www.britannica.com/shakespeare/micro/731/33.html.
A brief overview of the play with hyperlinks to character descriptions.

Bibliographies

Metz, G. Harold. *Four Plays Ascribed to Shakespeare: "The Reign of King Edward III," "Sir Thomas More," "The History of Cardenio," "The Two Noble Kinsmen: An Annotated Bibliography."* New York: Garland, 1982.

The Winter's Tale

Web Sites

"Study Questions for Shakespeare's *The Winter's Tale*." The Shakespeare Classroom. 26 June 2003, http://www.jetlink.net/~massij/wssq/winters.html.
Study questions for *The Winter's Tale*.

"*The Winter's Tale* by William Shakespeare." Ed. John Marwick. Feb. 2003. 30 June 2003, http://homepages.paradise.net.nz/~marlenn/.
A site devoted to *The Winter's Tale* made in conjunction with a community theater production of the play. Includes links to study notes, summaries, academic papers, and commentaries.

Biographies and Criticism

Hunt, Maurice. "*The Winter's Tale*": *Critical Essays.* New York: Garland, 1995.

Sanders, Wilbur. *The Winter's Tale.* Boston: Twayne, 1987.

James Shirley, 1596–1666

Web Sites

Devlin, William. "James Shirley." *Catholic Encyclopedia.* 8 June 2003, http://www.newadvent.org/cathen/16074a.htm.
A concise biography of Shirley reproduced from the 1908 *Catholic Encyclopedia.*

"James Shirley 1596–1666." *Luminarium.* 8 June 2003, http://www.luminarium.org/sevenlit/shirley/.
A comprehensive Web site on Shirley.

Neilson, W. A. "Ford and Shirley." *Bartleby.com.* 8 June 2003, http://www.bartleby.com/216/#8.
The entry on Shirley from *The Cambridge History of English and American Literature,* 1907–1921. Includes a biographical essay, as well as discussions of his work.

"Selected Poetry of James Shirley (1596–1666)." *Representative Poetry Online.* 8 June 2003, http://eir.library.utoronto.ca/rpo/display/poet299.html.
Full text of Shirley's "Cease, Warring Thoughts" and "The Glories of our Blood and State."

"Shirley, James." *Encyclopaedia Britannica Presents Shakespeare and the Globe: Then and Now."* 8 June 2003, http://www.britannica.com/shakespeare/micro/544/8.html.
A concise biography of Shirley.

Biographies and Criticism

Braden, Gordon. "James Shirley." Bowers, *Jacobean and Caroline Dramatists* (Dictionary of Literary Biography 58), 249–266.

Clark, Ira. *Professional Playwrights: Massinger, Ford, Shirley, & Brome.* Lexington, Ky.: UP Kentucky, 1992.

Lucow, Ben. *James Shirley.* Boston: Twayne, 1981.

Sanders, Julie. *Caroline Drama: The Plays of Massinger, Ford, Shirley, and Brome.* Plymouth, England: Northcote House, in association with the British Council, 1999.

Bibliographies

Zimmer, Ruth K. *James Shirley: A Reference Guide.* Boston: G. K. Hall, 1980.

Mary Sidney. See *Mary (Sidney) Herbert, Countess of Pembroke*

Sir Philip Sidney, 1554–1586

Web Sites

Atkins, J. W. H. "Renascence and Reformation." *Bartleby.com.* 6 June 2003, http://www.bartleby.com/213/#16.
Essays on Sidney and his *Arcadia* from *The Cambridge History of English and American Literature,* 1907–1921.

Lee, Sidney. "Sir Philip Sidney's *Astrophel and Stella.*" *Bartleby.com.* 8 June 2003, http://www.bartleby.com/213/1206.html.
An essay on Sidney's sonnet cycle *Astrophel and Stella* from *The Cambridge History of English and American Literature,* 1907–1921.

Renascence Editions. 8 June 2003, http://darkwing.uoregon.edu/~rbear/ren.htm.
Provides the full text of Sidney's *Astrophel and Stella* and *A Defence of Poesy.*

"Selected Poetry and Prose of Sir Philip Sidney (1554–1586)." *Representative Poetry Online.* 8 June 2003, http://eir.library.utoronto.ca/rpo/display/poet300.html.
Includes the full text of selected sonnets from Sidney's *Astrophel and Stella,* various other poems, and *The Defence of Poesy.*

"The Sidney Homepage." Ed. Gavin Alexander. 9 Sep. 2001. The University of Cambridge. 8 June 2003, http://www.english.cam.ac.uk/sidney/.
Home to the International Sidney Society, the Sidney-Spenser List, and the *Sidney Journal.* Features a detailed biography, a select bibliography of works on and by Sidney, and links to online editions of Sidney's works. Hosted by the Department of English at the University of Cambridge.

"Sir Philip Sidney (1554–1586)." *Luminarium.* 8 June 2003, http://www.luminarium.org/renlit/sidney.htm.
A comprehensive Sidney site.

"Sir Philip Sidney, *Astrophil and Stella.*" 8 June 2003, http://faculty.goucher.edu/eng211/sir_philip_sidney_.htm.
Reading notes and study prompts for Sidney's *Astrophel and Stella.*

"Sir Philip Sidney, Defense of Poesy." 8 June 2003, http://faculty.goucher.edu/eng211/sidneydefense_of_poesy.htm.
Reading notes and study prompts for Sidney's *Defence of Poesy.*

"Sir Philip Sidney, On Line." Eds. Donald Stump, C. Stuart Hunter, and Jerome S. Dees. Update unknown. Saint Louis University. 8 June 2003, http://www.slu.edu/colleges/AS/ENG/sidney/.

A comprehensive, annotated bibliography of writings by and about Sidney from 1554 through 1984, searchable through a user-friendly database. Also includes a helpful essay titled "About Sidney and Sidney Scholarship" by project director Professor Donald Stump of Saint Louis University. An invaluable tool for Sidney scholars.

Biographies and Criticism

Duncan-Jones, Katherine. *Sir Philip Sidney, Courtier Poet.* New Haven: Yale UP, 1991.

Garrett, Martin. *Sidney: The Critical Heritage.* London; New York: Routledge, 1996.

Hunt, Marvin. "Sir Philip Sidney." Richardson, *Sixteenth-Century British Nondramatic Writers,* 3d ser. (Dictionary of Literary Biography 167), 194–219.

Kay, Dennis. *Sir Philip Sidney: An Anthology of Modern Criticism.* Oxford: Clarendon P; New York: O UP, 1987.

Kimbrough, Robert. *Sir Philip Sidney.* New York: Twayne, 1971.

"Philip Sidney." *Literature Criticism from 1400 to 1800* 19: 316–435.
Excerpts of comments and criticism on Sidney from 1581–1991.

"Philip Sidney." *Literature Criticism from 1400 to 1800* 39: 197–300.
Excerpts of comments and criticism on Sidney from 1960–1996.

"Philip Sidney." *Poetry Criticism* 32: 213–337.
Excerpts of comments and criticism on Sidney from 1910–1996, with an annotated bibliography.

Indexes and Concordances

Donow, Herbert S., and Trevor J. Swanson. *A Concordance to the Poems of Sir Philip Sidney.* Ithaca: Cornell UP, 1975.
Based on William A. Ringler, Jr.'s *The Poems of Sir Philip Sidney* (New York: Oxford UP, 1962).

Journals

Sidney Journal. Guelph, Ontario: Department of English, University of Guelph, 1997–.
Continues *Sidney Newsletter & Journal* (1990–1997) and *Sidney Newsletter* (1980–1990). Tables of contents from 1998 to the present may be found online at http://www.english.cam.ac.uk/sidney/journal.htm.

Bibliographies

Guffey, George Robert. *Samuel Daniel, 1942–1965. Michael Drayton, 1941–1965. Sir Philip Sidney, 1941–1965.* London, Nether P, 1967.

Kinney Arthur F., et al. *Sidney in Retrospect: Selections from English Literary Renaissance.* Amherst: U Massachusetts P, 1988.

Kinney Arthur F. "Sir Philip Sidney." Hager, *Major Tudor Authors,* 419–428.
Brief biography, survey of major works and themes, critical reception, and bibliography of works by and about Sidney.

Stump, Donald V., Jerome S. Dees, and C. Stuart Hunter. *Sir Philip Sidney: An Annotated Bibliography of Texts and Criticism (1554–1984).* New York: G. K. Hall; Toronto: Maxwell Macmillan Canada; New York: Maxwell Macmillan International, 1994.

Washington, Mary A. *Sir Philip Sidney: An Annotated Bibliography of Modern Criticism, 1941–1970.* Columbia: U Missouri P, 1972.
Continues Tannenbaum's *Sir Philip Sidney (a Concise Bibliography),* 1941.

John Skelton, 1460?–1529

Web Sites

"1500—The Poetry of John Skelton." *Englishhistory.net.* 25 June 2003, http://englishhistory.net/tudor/skelton.html.
Provides the full text of "To Mistress Margaret Hussey," "To Mistress Isabell Pennell," "Lullay, Lullay, Like A Child," and "A Ballade of the Scottysshe Kynge."

"John Skelton (ca.1460–1529)." *Luminarium.* 8 June 2003, http://www.luminarium.org/renlit/skelton.htm.
A comprehensive Web site on Skelton.

"John Skelton & 'Skeltonics.' " 8 June 2003, http://athena.english.vt.edu/~jmooney/renmats/skelton.htm.
A brief look at Skeltonics.

"John Skelton Study Questions." 8 June 2003, http://smith.hanover.edu/sqskelton.html.
Brief study prompts for Skelton's poems including "Lullay, Lullay, Like a Child" and "Mannerly Margery, Milk and Ale." Keyed to the *Longman Anthology of British Literature,* 2d ed.

Koelbing, Arthur. "Barclay and Skelton." *Bartleby.com.* 8 June 2003, http://www.bartleby.com/213/index.html#4.
Essays on Skelton's life and works from *The Cambridge History of English and American Literature: An Encyclopedia in Eighteen Volumes,* 1907–1921.

"Poems of John Skelton." Ed. Ray Siemens and Greg Waite. 21 Aug. 2001. Malaspina University-College. 8 June 2003, http://web.mala.bc.ca/siemensr/teaching/Engl359-01-Skelton.htm.
Contains the full text of Skelton's "Agaynste a Comely Coystrowne," "The Bowge of Courte," "A Lawde and Prayse," and "A Ballade of the Scottysshe Kynge."

"Selected Poetry of John Skelton (1460?–1529)." *Representative Poetry Online.* 8 June 2003, http://eir.library.utoronto.ca/rpo/display/poet301.html.
Contains the full text of Skelton's "The Book of Philip Sparrow" and "The Tunning of Elenor Rumming."

Biographies and Criticism

Carpenter, Nan Cooke. *John Skelton.* New York: Twayne, 1967.

"John Skelton." *Literature Criticism from 1400 to 1800* 71: 243–394.
    Excerpts of comments and criticism on Skelton from 1935–1998.

"John Skelton." *Poetry Criticism* 25: 327–402.
    Excerpts of comments and criticism on Skelton from 1935–1996, with an annotated bibliography.

Kinney, Arthur F. "John Skelton." Richardson, *Sixteenth-Century British Nondramatic Writers,* 2d ser. (Dictionary of Literary Biography 136), 299–316.

Indexes and Concordances

Fox, Alistair and Gregory Waite. *A Concordance to the Complete English Poems of John Skelton.* Ithaca: Cornell UP, 1987.
    Based on John Scattergood's edition of *John Skelton: The Complete English Poems* (New Haven: Yale UP, 1983).

Bibliographies

Hager, Alan. "John Skelton." Hager, *Major Tudor Authors,* 431–435.
    Brief biography, survey of major works and themes, critical reception, and bibliography of works by and about Skelton.

Kinsman, Robert S. *John Skelton, Early Tudor Laureate: An Annotated Bibliography, c. 1488–1977.* Boston: G. K. Hall, 1979.

Captain John Smith, 1580–1631

Web Sites

Brown, Boyd. "Life of Captain John Smith." *Jamestown Historic Briefs.* 21 Mar. 2002. National Park Service. 8 June 2003, http://www.nps.gov/colo/Jthanout/JSmith.html.
    A biography of John Smith from the Web site of the Colonial National Historical Park.

"Captain John Smith, *The Generall Historie of Virginia, New England & the Summer Isles* (1624)." History 41: The American Colonies. Ed. Bruce Dorsey. Update unknown. Swarthmore College. 8 June 2003, http://www.swarthmore.edu/SocSci/bdorsey1/41docs/10-smi.html.
    Selections from Smith's book *The Generall Historie of Virginia.*

"John Smith (1580–1631)." English 310/510: Early American Literature. Ed. Donna M. Campbell. 8 Jan. 2003. Gonzaga University. 8 June 2003, http://guweb2.gonzaga.edu/faculty/campbell/enl310/smith.htm.
    A site devoted to John Smith. Includes links to articles on Smith.

Biographies and Criticism

"(Captain) John Smith." *Literature Criticism from 1400 to 1800* 9: 347–389.
Excerpts of comments and criticism on Smith from 1624–1980.

Emerson, Everett H. *Captain John Smith.* New York: Twayne; Toronto: Maxwell Macmillan Canada; New York: Maxwell Macmillan International, 1993.

Fleming, Thomas. "John Smith." Wilson, *American Historians, 1607–1865* (Dictionary of Literary Biography 30), 285–290.

Leary, Lewis. "John Smith." Elliott, *American Colonial Writers, 1606–1734* (Dictionary of Literary Biography 24), 289–293.

Bibliographies

Hayes, Kevin J. *Captain John Smith: A Reference Guide.* Boston: G. K. Hall, 1991.

Saint Robert Southwell, 1561?–1595

Web Sites

Child, Harold H. "Robert Southwell." *Bartleby.com.* 8 June 2003, http://www.bartleby.com/214/0701.html.
An essay on the life and works of Southwell from *The Cambridge History of English and American Literature,* 1907–1921.

"Robert Southwell (1561–1595)." *Luminarium.* 8 June 2003, http://www.luminarium.org/renlit/southwell.htm.
A comprehensive Web site on Southwell.

Thurston, Herbert. "Venerable Robert Southwell." *Catholic Encyclopedia.* 8 June 2003, http://www.newadvent.org/cathen/14164a.htm.
A concise biography of Southwell reproduced from the 1908 *Catholic Encyclopedia.*

Biographies and Criticism

Brownlow, F. W. *Robert Southwell.* New York: Twayne, 1996.

———. "Robert Southwell." Richardson, *Sixteenth-Century British Nondramatic Writers,* 3d ser. (Dictionary of Literary Biography 167), 220–227.

Cousins, A. D. *The Catholic Religious Poets from Southwell to Crashaw: A Critical History.* London: Sheed & Ward, 1991.

Bibliographies

Bouchard, Gary. "Robert Southwell." Hager, *Major Tudor Authors,* 435–438.
Brief biography, survey of major works and themes, critical reception, and bibliography of works by and about Southwell.

Edmund Spenser, c. 1552–1599

"Study Questions for Edmund Spenser's *The Faerie Queene,* Book I." 8 June 2003, http://english.sxu.edu/boyer/201_rdg_qsts/fq1_sels_n7_qst.htm.
Study questions for Book I of Spenser's *Faerie Queene.*

Courthope, W. J. "The Poetry of Spenser." *Bartleby.com.* 8 June 2003, http://www.bartleby.com/213/index.html#11.
The entry on Spenser from *The Cambridge History of English and American Literature,* 1907–1921. Includes various biographical and critical essays.

"Edmund Spenser." ENG310A: English Literature to 1660. Ed. M. Teresa Tavormina. 16 Mar. 1999. Michigan State University. 8 June 2003, http://clcgi.cl.msu.edu/~tavrmina/eng310a/PPT/spenser/.
A brief PowerPoint presentation on Book I of Spenser's *Faerie Queene.*

"Edmund Spenser." Update unknown. *Merchant Taylor's School.* 8 June 2003, http://www.mtsn.org.uk/omts/spenser.htm.
A concise biography of Spenser from the Web site of the Merchant Taylor's School, where he attended in his youth.

"Edmund Spenser (1552–1599)." *Luminarium.* 8 June 2003, http://www.luminarium.org/renlit/spenser.htm.
A comprehensive Web site on Spenser. Provides links to online texts of Spenser, critical essays and articles, and to a brief biography.

"Edmund Spenser, *Amoretti* and 'Epithalamion.' " 8 June 2003, http://faculty.goucher.edu/eng211/.
Review notes for Spenser's *Amoretti* sonnet cycle and his "Epithalamion."

The Edmund Spenser Home Page. Ed. Andrew Zurcher. 1 Jan. 2000. University of Cambridge. 8 June 2003, http://www.english.cam.ac.uk/spenser/main.htm.
Hosted by the Department of English at the University of Cambridge, this site is the most comprehensive Spenser site found on the Web. Contains a biography, chronology, links to online texts, and a forthcoming comprehensive bibliography of Spenser criticism. Home to the International Spenser Society and the journal *Spenser Studies.*

"Edmund Spenser: Study Questions." 8 June 2003, http://smith.hanover.edu/sqspenser.html.
Study questions for Spenser's "Epithalamion" and *Amoretti.* Keyed to the *Longman Anthology of British Literature,* 2d ed.

Renascence Editions. 8 June 2003, http://darkwing.uoregon.edu/%7Ebear/ren.htm#spen.
Contains the full texts of the works of Edmund Spenser. Of considerable interest is the online version of *The Shepheardes Calender,* which includes the glosses and woodcuts that accompanied the earliest printings of the text.

"Review Notes for *The Faerie Queene,* Book I." Ed. J. M. Richardson. Update unknown. Lakehead University. 8 June 2003, http://flash.lakeheadu.ca/~jrichard/fq.html.
A helpful, detailed set of review notes for Book I of Spenser's *Faerie Queene.*

"Selected Poetry of Edmund Spenser (1552–1599)." *Representative Poetry Online.* 8 June 2003, http://eir.library.utoronto.ca/rpo/display/poet308.html.
   Contains the text of selected sonnets from *Amoretti,* the complete Book I of *The Faerie Queene,* excerpts from Books II, III, and VI, "April" and "October" of *The Shepheardes Calender,* and other minor works.

Biographies and Criticism

"Age of Spenser." *Literature Criticism from 1400 to 1800* 39: 1–70.
   An introduction to and comments and criticism regarding the literary period referred to as "The Age of Spenser."

"Edmund Spenser." *Literature Criticism from 1400 to 1800* 5: 290–368.
   Excerpts of comments and criticism on Spenser from 1579–1986.

"Edmund Spenser." *Literature Criticism from 1400 to 1800* 39: 301–397.
   Excerpts of comments and criticism on Spenser from 1889–1987.

"Edmund Spenser." *Poetry Criticism* 8: 321–400.
   Excerpts of comments and criticism on Spenser from 1589–1979, with an annotated bibliography.

Hadfield, Andrew, Ed. *Edmund Spenser.* New York: Longman, 1996.

Oram, William A. *Edmund Spenser.* New York: Twayne; London: Prentice Hall International, 1997.

Stump, Donald V. "Edmund Spenser." Richardson, *Sixteenth-Century British Nondramatic Writers,* 3d ser. (Dictionary of Literary Biography 167), 228–263.

Suzuki, Mihoko. *Critical Essays on Edmund Spenser.* New York: G.K. Hall, 1996.

Dictionaries, Encyclopedias, and Handbooks

Hadfield, Andrew. *The Cambridge Companion to Spenser.* Cambridge and New York: Cambridge UP, 2001.

Hamilton, A. C. *The Spenser Encyclopedia.* Toronto: U Toronto P, 1990.

Heale, Elizabeth. *The Faerie Queene: A Reader's Guide.* Cambridge and New York: Cambridge UP, 1987.

Maley, Willy. *A Spenser Chronology.* Lanham, Md.: Macmillan; Barnes & Noble, 1994.

Nohrnberg, James. *The Analogy of The Faerie Queene.* Princeton: Princeton UP, 1976.

Indexes and Concordances

Osgood, Charles Grosvenor, ed. *A Concordance to the Poems of Edmund Spenser.* Washington, D.C.: Carnegie Institution of Washington, 1915. Reissued Gloucester: P. Smith, 1963.
   Based on Morris and Hales's *Complete Works* (London: Macmillan, 1869), Dodge's *Complete Poetical Works* (Boston: Houghton Mifflin, 1907), and De Selincourt's *Poetical Works* (London: Oxford UP, 1910).

Whitman, Charles Huntington. *A Subject-Index to the Poems of Edmund Spenser.* New Haven: Yale UP, 1918.

Journals

Spenser Newsletter. Amherst: U Western Ontario; Renaissance Society of America; U of Massachusetts, Amherst; Holyoke Community C, 1970–.

Spenser Studies. Pittsburgh, Pennsylvania: U Pittsburgh P., 1980–.
Indexed online at http://www.english.cam.ac.uk/spenser/studies.htm.

Bibliographies

Carpenter, Frederic Ives. *A Reference Guide to Edmund Spenser.* New York: Kraus Reprint, 1969.
A reprint of the first edition by the University of Chicago Press, 1923. The first edition was updated by Atkinson, Dorothy F. *Edmund Spenser, a Bibliographical Supplement.* Baltimore: Johns Hopkins P, 1937.

Frushell, Richard C. *Contemporary Thought on Edmund Spenser: With a Bibliography of Criticism of the Faerie Queene, 1900–1970.* Carbondale: Southern Illinois UP, 1975.

Kaske, Carol V. "Edmund Spenser." Hager, *Major Tudor Authors,* 438–446.
Brief biography, survey of major works and themes, critical reception, and bibliography of works by and about Spenser.

McNeir, Waldo F. and Foster Provost. *Edmund Spenser: An Annotated Bibliography, 1937–1972.* Pittsburgh: Duquesne UP; Atlantic Highlands: distributed by Humanities P, 1975.

William Strode, 1600–1645

Web Sites

"Selected Poetry of William Strode (1602–1645)." *Representative Poetry Online.* 8 June 2003, http://eir.library.utoronto.ca/rpo/display/poet315.html.
The full text of "On Chloris Walking in the Snow," attributed to Strode.

"University Plays: Barten Holiday's *Technogamia;* Allegorical and satirical character of the later Plays." *Bartleby.com.* 8 June 2003, http://www.bartleby.com/216/1223.html.
This essay on University Plays includes a brief discussion of Strode's play *The Floating Island.* From *The Cambridge History of English and American Literature,* 1907–1921.

Biographies and Criticism

Miller, Edmund. "William Strode." Hester, *Seventeenth-Century British Nondramatic Poets,* 2d ser. (Dictionary of Literary Biography 126), 250–255.

Strode, William. *The Poetical Works of William Strode.* Ed. Bertram Dobell. London: Published by the editor, 1907.
 The only modern edition of Strode's work, contains a biography and some critical annotations.

Sir John Suckling, 1609–1642

Web Sites

Bayne, Ronald. "Lesser Jacobean and Caroline Dramatists: Sir John Suckling's Plays: *Aglaura, The Goblins,* and *Brennoralt.*" *Bartleby.com.* 8 June 2003, http://www.bartleby.com/216/0921.html.
 An essay on Suckling's drama from *The Cambridge History of English and American Literature,* 1907–1921.

Moorman, F. W. "Cavalier Lyrists: Sir John Suckling." *Bartleby.com.* 8 June. 2003, http://www.bartleby.com/217/0110.html.
 An essay on Suckling's poetry from *The Cambridge History of English and American Literature,* 1907–1921.

"Selected Poetry of Sir John Suckling (1609–1642)." *Representative Poetry Online.* 8 June 2003, http://eir.library.utoronto.ca/rpo/display/poet316.html.
 The full text of several Suckling poems, including "Out upon it, I have lov'd" and "Why so pale and wan fond lover?" Includes biographical information.

"Sir John Suckling (1609–1642)." *Luminarium.* 8 June 2003, http://www.luminarium.org/sevenlit/suckling/.
 A comprehensive Web site on Suckling.

Biographies and Criticism

"John Suckling." *Literature Criticism from 1400 to 1800* 75: 293–373.
 Excerpts of comments and criticism on Suckling from 1932–1995.

"Sir John Suckling." *Poetry Criticism* 30: 116–165.
 Excerpts of comments and criticism on Suckling from 1910–1982, with an annotated bibliography.

Shawcross, John T. "Sir John Suckling." Hester, *Seventeenth-Century British Nondramatic Poets,* 2d ser. (Dictionary of Literary Biography 126), 256–263.

Squier, Charles L. *Sir John Suckling.* Boston: Twayne, 1978.

———. "Sir John Suckling." Bowers, *Jacobean and Caroline Dramatists* (Dictionary of Literary Biography 58), 267–276.

Henry Howard, Surrey, Earl of.
See *Henry Howard, Earl of Surrey*

Jeremy Taylor, 1613–1667

Web Sites

Hutton, W. H. "Caroline Divines: Jeremy Taylor." *Bartleby.com.* 8 June 2003,
http://www.bartleby.com/217/0624.html.
    An essay on the life and works of Taylor from *The Cambridge History of English and American Literature,* 1907–1921.

"Jeremy Taylor, Bishop and Theologian, 13 August 1667." *James Kiefer's Christian Biographies.* Ed. James Kiefer. Update unknown. Rowan University. 8 June 2003,
http://elvis.rowan.edu/~kilroy/JEK/08/13.html.
    A brief biography of Taylor.

"Taylor, Jeremy (1613–1667)." *Christian Classics Ethereal Library.* 8 June 2003,
http://www.ccel.org/t/taylor/.
    Features full text of Taylor's *Rule and Exercises of Holy Living* and *Rule and Exercises of Holy Dying* in rich text format. Also includes biographical essays.

Biographies and Criticism

Miller, Edmund. "Jeremy Taylor." Lein, *British Prose Writers of the Early Seventeenth Century* (Dictionary of Literary Biography 151), 294–305.

Bibliographies

Gathorne-Hardy, Robert, and William Proctor Williams. *A Bibliography of the Writings of Jeremy Taylor to 1700, with a Section of Tayloriana.* Dekalb: Northern Illinois UP, 1971.

Williams, William Proctor. *Jeremy Taylor, 1700–1976: An Annotated Checklist.* New York: Garland, 1979.

John Taylor, 1580–1653

Web Sites

Aldis, H. G. "John Taylor, the Thames Waterman." *Bartleby.com.* 8 June 2003,
http://www.bartleby.com/214/1812.html.
    A biographical essay on Taylor from *The Cambridge History of English and American Literature,* 1907–1921.

"The Praise of Hemp-Seed." *Renascence Editions.* Ed. Joanne Gates. 8 June 2003,
http://darkwing.uoregon.edu/%7Erbear/taylor1.html.
    The full text of Taylor's poem "The Praise of Hemp-Seed."

Biographies and Criticism

Capp, B. S. *The World of John Taylor, the Water-Poet, 1578–1653.* Oxford: Clarendon P; New York: Oxford UP, 1994.

Panek, Patricia. "John Taylor." Hester, *Seventeenth-Century British Nondramatic Poets,* 1st ser. (Dictionary of Literary Biography 121), 255–263.

Cyril Tourneur, 1575?–1626

Web Sites

"Study Questions for Cyril Tourneur's *The Revenger's Tragedy* (1607)." *Jacobean Drama.* 8 June 2003, http://www.jetlink.net/~massij/jacob/rt.htm.
Study questions for *The Revenger's Tragedy*, sometimes attributed to Tourneur.

"Tourneur, Cyril." *Encyclopaedia Britannica Presents Shakespeare and the Globe: Then and Now.* 8 June 2003, http://www.britannica.com/shakespeare/micro/600/45.html.
A brief biography of Tourneur.

Vaughan, C. E. "Tourneur and Webster." *Bartleby.com.* 8 June 2003, http://www.bartleby.com/216/index.html#7.
The entry on Tourneur from volume six of *The Cambridge History of English and American Literature*, 1907–1921. Includes a biography and commentary on his works.

Biographies and Criticism

Cantor, Paul A. "Cyril Tourneur." Bowers, *Jacobean and Caroline Dramatists* (Dictionary of Literary Biography 58), 277–283.

"Cyril Tourneur." *Literature Criticism from 1400 to 1800* 66: 269–365.
Excerpts of comments and criticism on Tourneur from 1930–1994.

Schuman, Samuel. *Cyril Tourneur.* Boston: Twayne, 1977.

White, Martin. *Middleton and Tourneur.* New York: St. Martin's, 1992.

Bibliographies

Donovan, Dennis G. *Thomas Dekker, 1945–1965; Thomas Heywood, 1938–1965; Cyril Tourneur, 1945–1965.* London: Nether P, 1967.

Tucker, Kenneth. *A Bibliography of Writings By and About John Ford and Cyril Tourneur.* Boston: G. K. Hall, 1977.

Anna Trapnel, fl. 1654–1660

Web Sites

"Renaissance Women Online." *The Brown University Women Writers Project.* 8 Jun 2003, http://textbase.wwp.brown.edu:1084/dynaweb/wwptextbase/wwpRWO/.
Scroll down to "Trapnel" for links to the full text of "The Cry of a Stone" and "Strange and Wonderful News."

"Strange and Wonderful Newes from White-Hall: or, The Mighty Visions Proceeding from Mistris Anna Trapnel." *The Emory Women Writers Resource Project*. 8 June 2003, http://chaucer.library.emory.edu/cgi-bin/sgml2html/wwrp.pl.
Scroll down to "Trapnel" to link to the text.

William Tyndale, c. 1495–1536

Web Sites

The Tyndale Society Home Page. Ed. D. Pollard. Update unknown. The Tyndale Society. 8 June 2003, http://www.tyndale.org/.
Home of the Tyndale Society this site includes a comprehensive biography, a Tyndale genealogy, announcements pertaining to Tyndale and other Reformation topics, and links to Tyndale related sites.

"The William Tyndale Home Page." *Friends of William Tyndale/History of the English Bible*. Update unknown. 8 June 2003, http://www.williamtyndale.com/.
Includes the life and martyrdom of Tyndale from John Foxe's *Book Of Martyrs*, A William Tyndale and Reformation timeline, Tyndale image galleries, and a history of the English Bible.

Biographies and Criticism

Daniell, David. *William Tyndale: A Biography*. New Haven: Yale UP, 1994.

Day, John T. "William Tyndale." Richardson, *Sixteenth-Century British Nondramatic Writers,* 1st ser. (Dictionary of Literary Biography 132), 296–311.

Journals

Reformation. Oxford: Tyndale Society, 1996–.

Bibliographies

Hansard-Weiner, Sonja, and Andrew D. Weiner. "William Tyndale." Hager, *Major Tudor Authors,* 459–465.
A brief biography, survey of major works and themes, critical reception, and bibliography of works by and about Tyndale.

Nicholas Udall, c. 1505–1556

Web Sites

Boas, F. S. "The Drama to 1642, Part One." *Bartleby.com*. 8 June 2003, http://www.bartleby.com/215/.
Scroll down to "V. Early English Comedy" for links to essays: "Nicholas Udall" and "*Ralph Roister Doister*." From *The Cambridge History of English and American Literature,* 1907–1921.

Caputo, Nicoletta. "Udall, Nicholas. (1505–1556)." *Literary Encyclopedia and Literary Dictionary*. Ed. and update unknown. 8 June 2003, http://www.litencyc. com/php/speople.php?rec=true&UID=4498.
A concise biography of Udall.

Early Tudor Texts. 8 June 2003, http://www.chass.utoronto.ca/datalib/codebooks/ utm/tudor.htm.
Links to the full text of Udall's *Ralph Roister Doister*. Note: the ASCII tags sometimes makes the text slightly difficult to read.

Biographies and Criticism

Axton, Marie. "Nicholas Udall." Bowers, *Elizabethan Dramatists* (Dictionary of Literary Biography 62), 354–360.

Henry Vaughan, 1621–1695

Web Sites

"Henry Vaughan (1621–1695)." 8 June 2003, http://www.luminarium.org/sevenlit/ vaughan/.
A comprehensive Web site on Vaughan.

Hutchinson, F. E. "The Sacred Poets." *Bartleby.com.* 8 June 2003, http://www. bartleby.com/217/index.html#2.
Several essays on Vaughan from *The Cambridge History of English and American Literature,* 1907–1921.

"Selected Poetry of Henry Vaughan (1622?–1695)." *Representative Poetry Online.* 8 June 2003, http://eir.library.utoronto.ca/rpo/display/poet338.html.
Selections of Vaughan's poetry including "They Are All Gone into the World of Light" and "Christ's Nativity."

Biographies and Criticism

Friedenreich, Kenneth. *Henry Vaughan.* Boston: Twayne, 1978.

"Henry Vaughan." *Literature Criticism from 1400 to 1800* 27: 288–398.
Excerpts of comments and criticism on Vaughan from 1651–1990.

Wall, John N. "Henry Vaughan." Hester, *Seventeenth-Century British Nondramatic Poets,* 3d ser. (Dictionary of Literary Biography 131), 291–309.

Indexes and Concordances

Tuttle, Imilda. *Concordance to Vaughan's Silex Scintillans.* University Park: Pennsylvania State UP, 1969
Based on French Fogle's edition of *The Complete Poetry of Henry Vaughan* (Garden City, N.Y.: Doubleday 1964).

Bibliographies

Marilla, Esmond Linworth. *A Comprehensive Bibliography of Henry Vaughan*. New York: Haskell House, 1972.
 A reprint of the first edition by the University of Alabama Press, 1948. Supplemented by: Esmond Linworth Marilla and James D. Simmonds's *Henry Vaughan: A Bibliographical Supplement, 1946–1960* (U Alabama P, 1963).

Edmund Waller, 1606–1687

Web Sites

"Edmund Waller (1606–1687)." *Luminarium*. 8 June 2003, http://www.luminarium. org/sevenlit/waller/.
 A comprehensive Web site on Waller.

"Samuel Johnson's Life of Edmund Waller." *The Penn State Archive of Samuel Johnson's Lives of the Poets*. 8 June 2003, http://www.hn.psu.edu/Faculty/ KKemmerer/poets/waller/life.htm.
 The full text of Johnson's life of Waller.

"Selected Poetry of Edmund Waller (1606–1687)." *Representative Poetry Online*. 8 June 2003, http://eir.library.utoronto.ca/rpo/display/poet341.html.
 The full text of the following Waller poems: "Of the Last Verses in the Book," "On a Girdle," "The Self Banished," "Song: Go Lovely Rose," "The Story of Phoebus and Daphne, Applied," and "To the King on his Navy."

Thompson, A. Hamilton. "Writers of the Couplet: Edmund Waller." *Bartleby.com*. 8 June 2003, http://www.bartleby.com/217/0304.html.
 An essay on the life and poetry of Waller from *The Cambridge History of English and American Literature,* 1907–1921.

Biographies and Criticism

Donnelly, M. L. "Edmund Waller." Hester, *Seventeenth-Century British Nondramatic Poets,* 2d ser. (Dictionary of Literary Biography 126), 264–285.

Izaak Walton, 1593–1683

Web Sites

"*The Complete Angler*, Izaak Walton and Charles Cotton." *Renascence Editions*. 3 June 2003, http://www.uoregon.edu/~rbear/walton/.
 The full text of Walton's *The Complete Angler*.

"Izaak Walton 1593–1683." *Literary Heritage West Midlands*. 28 Oct. 2002. 8 June 2003, http://www3.shropshire-cc.gov.uk/walton.htm.
 A profile of Walton with a bibliography of his works.

Biographies and Criticism

"Izaak Walton." *Literature Criticism from 1400 to 1800* 72: 225–363.
Excerpts of comments and criticism on Walton from 1819–1998.

Lein, Clayton D. "Izaak Walton." Lein, *British Prose Writers of the Early Seventeenth Century,* (Dictionary of Literary Biography 151), 306–321.

Naiman, Sandra. "Izaak Walton." Baker and Womack, *Pre-Nineteenth-Century British Book Collectors and Bibliographers,* (Dictionary of Literary Biography 213), 386–393.

Stanwood, P. G. *Izaak Walton.* New York: Twayne; London: Prentice Hall International, 1998.

Bibliographies

Horne, Bernard S. *The Compleat Angler, 1653–1967; A New Bibliography.* Pittsburgh: Pittsburgh Bibliophiles; distributed by the U of Pittsburgh P, 1970.

John Webster, c. 1578–c. 1626

Web Sites

"*The Duchess of Malfi.*" Ed. Larry Brown. 27 Jan. 2003. 8 June 2003, http://larryavisbrown.homestead.com/files/Malfi/malfi_home.htm.
Contains the full text of Webster's *The Duchess of Malfi.*

"*The Duchess of Malfi*" 14 Sep. 1998. *John Webster Resource Page.* 8 June 2003, http://www.fortunecity.com/victorian/dali/88/index.htm.
A helpful site created by a student at the National University of Singapore. Content includes character analyses, themes, historical sources of the *The Duchess of Malfi*, and information on John Webster.

"John Webster's *The Duchess of Malfi.*" Ed. and update unknown. 8 June 2003, http://wspanic75.tripod.com/webster.html.
Contains a biography of Webster, an overview of trends in scholarship, and an annotated bibliography of critical works on Webster's *The Duchess of Malfi.*

"John Webster." *Luminarium.* 8 June 2003, http://www.luminarium.org/sevenlit/webster/.
A comprehensive Web site on Webster.

"Reading Questions for John Webster's *The Duchess of Malfi.*" 8 June 2003, http://english.sxu.edu/boyer/201_rdg_qsts/dmalfi_n7_qst.htm.
Reading questions for Webster's *The Duchess of Malfi* arranged by act and scene.

"Study Questions for Webster's *The Duchess of Malfi* (1613–14)." *Jacobean Drama.* 8 June 2003, http://www.jetlink.net/~massij/jacob/malfi.htm.
Study questions for *The Duchess of Malfi.*

Vaughan, C. E. "Tourneur and Webster." *Bartleby.com*. 8 June 2003, http://www.
bartleby.com/216/index.html#7.
    The entry on Webster from *The Cambridge History of English and American Literature*, 1907–1921. Includes a biography and commentary on his works.

Biographies and Criticism

Hammond, Antony. "John Webster." Bowers, *Jacobean and Caroline Dramatists* (Dictionary of Literary Biography 58), 284–302.

"John Webster." *Drama Criticism* 2: 420–468.
    Excerpts of criticism on Webster in general and on *The White Devil* and *The Duchess of Malfi* from 1919–1973, with an annotated bibliography.

"John Webster." *Literature Criticism from 1400 to 1800* 33: 331–404.
    Excerpts of comments and criticism on Webster from 1949–1995.

Ranald, Margaret Loftus. *John Webster*. Boston: Twayne, 1989.

Wymer, Rowland. *Webster and Ford*. New York: St. Martin's, 1995.

Indexes and Concordances

Corballis, Richard, and J. M. Harding. *A Concordance to the Works of John Webster*.
Salzburg: Institut für Englische Sprache und Literatur, Universität Salzburg, 1978.
    Based on F. L. Lucas's *The Complete Works of John Webster* (Cambridge: Cambridge UP, 1966).

Bibliographies

Mahaney, William E. *John Webster: A Classified Bibliography*. Salzburg: Inst. f. Engl.
Sprache u. Literatur, U Salzburg, 1973.

Schuman, Samuel. *John Webster: A Reference Guide*. Boston: G. K. Hall, 1985.

Isabella Whitney, fl. 1567–c. 1573

Web Sites

"Isabella Whitney." Ed. Michael Best. 8 June 2003, http://web.uvic.ca/shakespeare/
Library/SLT/literature/whitney.html.
    A brief introduction to Whitney with examples of her poetry.

"Study Questions for Isabella Whitney." 8 June 2003, http://smith.hanover.
edu/sqwhitney.html.
    Study questions for Whitney's "I.W. To Her Unconstant Lover," "The Admonition by the Author," and "A Careful Complaint."

"*A Sweet Nosegay*." *Early Modern Women Writers*. Ed. and update unknown. Montana
State University. 8 June 2003, http://www.montana.edu/wwwwhitn/index.html.
    An electronic edition of Whitney's poetry collection, *A Sweet Nosegay* (1573).

Biographies and Criticism

Travitsky, Betty S. "Isabella Whitney." Richardson, *Sixteenth-Century British Nondramatic Writers* (Dictionary of Literary Biography 136), 341–344.

Thomas Wilson, c. 1523–1581

Web Sites

"*The Arte of Rhetorique.*" *Renascence Editions.* 8 June 2003, http://www.uoregon.edu/~rbear/arte/arte.htm.
  Provides the full text of Wilson's *The Arte of Rhetoric.*

"Sir Thomas Wilson (1524–1581)." Ed. Nicholas Sharp. 25 Apr. 2003. Virginia Commonwealth University. 8 June 2003, http://www.people.vcu.edu/~nsharp/wilshme1.htm.
  A good introductory site to Thomas Wilson. Includes a biography and a summary and full text of books I and II of *The Art of Rhetoric* (abridged and modernized).

Biographies and Criticism

Baumlin, Tita French. "Thomas Wilson." Malone, *British Rhetoricians and Logicians, 1500–1660,* 1st ser. (Dictionary of Literary Biography 236), 282–306.

Henderson, Judith Rice. "Thomas Wilson." Richardson, *Sixteenth-Century British Nondramatic Writers,* 1st ser. (Dictionary of Literary Biography 132), 340–345.

Medine, Peter E. *Thomas Wilson.* Boston: Twayne, 1986.

Bibliographies

Kennedy, William J. "Thomas Wilson." Hager, *Major Tudor Authors*, 470–473.
  Brief biography, survey of major works and themes, critical reception, and bibliography of works by and about Wilson.

George Wither, 1588–1667

Web Sites

De Sélincourt, Hugh. "The Successors of Spenser: George Wither." *Bartleby.com.* 8 June 2003, http://www.bartleby.com/214/0902.html.
  An essay on the life and works of Wither from *The Cambridge History of English and American Literature,* 1907–1921.

"George Wither: *A Collection of Emblemes,* etc." *The English Emblem Book Project.* Ed. Roberta Astroff. Update unknown. Penn State University Libraries. 8 June 2003, http://emblem.libraries.psu.edu/.
  A scanned version of the 1635 edition of Wither's *Collection of Emblems.*

"Selected Poetry of George Wither (1588–1667)." *Representative Poetry Online*. 8 June
    2003, http://eir.library.utoronto.ca/rpo/display/poet361.html.
    The full text of Wither's "A Christmas Carol," "The Marigold," and "Shall I Wast-
ing in Despair."

Biographies and Criticism

Doelman, James. "George Wither." Hester, *Seventeenth-Century British Nondramatic
    Poets,* 1st ser. (Dictionary of Literary Biography 121), 273–286.

Sir Henry Wotton, 1568–1639

Web Sites

"The Life of Sir Henry Wotton by Izaak Walton." *Project Canterbury*. Ed. Irene C. Teas.
    Update unknown. Society of Archbishop Justus. 8 June 2003, http://justus.anglican.
    org/resources/pc/walton/wotton.html.
    The full text of Walton's life of Wotton.

"Selected Poetry of Sir Henry Wotton (1568–1639)." *Representative Poetry Online*. 8
    June 2003, http://eir.library.utoronto.ca/rpo/display/poet365.html.
    The full text of Wotton's "The Character of a Happy Life" and "You Meaner Beau-
ties of the Night."

Biographies and Criticism

"Henry Wotton." *Literature Criticism from 1400 to 1800* 68: 331–389.
    Excerpts of comments and criticism on Wotton from 1651–1984.

Pebworth, Ted-Larry. "Sir Henry Wotton." Hester, *Seventeenth-Century British
    Nondramatic Poets,* 1st ser. (Dictionary of Literary Biography 121), 286–295.

Lady Mary Wroth, 1587–1651?

Web Sites

"Lady Mary Wroth, 1584–1653." *Luminarium*. 8 June 2003, http://www.luminarium.
    org/sevenlit/wroth/.
    A comprehensive Web site on Wroth.

"Lady Mary Wroth." *As One Phoenix: Four Seventeenth Century Women Poets*. 8 June
    2003, http://www.usask.ca/english/phoenix/wrothm.htm.
    Features an inclusive bibliography of editions and critical studies. Also includes
biography and selected poems. Maintained by Professor Ron Cooley at the University of
Saskatchewan.

"Lady Mary Wroth." *CERES: The Sidney Home Page*. Ed. Nandini Das. 15 June 2001.
    University of Cambridge. 8 June 2003, http://www.english.cam.ac.uk/wroth/.
    Provides a biography, bibliography, e-texts, and links to Wroth-related pages.

"Lady Mary Wroth, *The Countess of Montgomery's Urania* and *Pamphilia to Amphialanthus.*" 8 June 2003, http://faculty.goucher.edu/eng211/lady_mary_wroth.htm.
Study notes and questions for Wroth's *The Countess of Montgomery's Urania* and *Pamphilia to Amphialanthus.*

"Mary Wroth: Bibliography." *Female Dramatists of the English Seventeenth Century.* 8 June 2003, http://english.uwaterloo.ca/courses/engl710b/wrothbib.html.
A bibliography of critical works on Wroth.

Biographies and Criticism

"Lady Mary Wroth." *Literature Criticism from 1400 to 1800* 30: 329–401.
Excerpts of criticism on Wroth from 1946 to 1993, with an annotated bibliography.

Miller, Naomi J., and Gary Waller, eds. *Reading Mary Wroth: Representing Alternatives in Early Modern England.* Knoxville: U Tennessee P, 1991.

Roberts, Josephine A. "Lady Mary Wroth." Hester, *Seventeenth-Century British Nondramatic Poets,* 1st ser. (Dictionary of Literary Biography 121), 296–309.

Walker, Kim. " 'This Strang Labourinth': Lady Mary Wroth." *Women Writers of the English Renaissance.* New York: Twayne, 1996, 170–190.

Bibliographies

Dellaria, Anita. "Lady Mary Wroth." Hager, *Major Tudor Authors,* 473–476.
Brief biography, survey of major works and themes, critical reception, and bibliography of works by and about Wroth.

Sir Thomas Wyatt, 1503–1542

Web Sites

"Renascence and Reformation." *Bartleby.com.* 8 June 2003, http://www.bartleby.com/213/.
Scroll down to "VIII. The New English Poetry" for links to the following essays: "Sir Thomas Wyatt," "Wyatt's sonnets," "Wyatt's treatment of love," and "Wyatt's epigrams, satires and devotional pieces." From *The Cambridge History of English and American Literature*, 1907–1921.

"Sir Thomas Wyatt (1503–1542)." *Luminarium.* 8 June 2003, http://www.luminarium.org/renlit/wyatt.htm.
A comprehensive Web site on Wyatt.

"Sir Thomas Wyatt: Study Questions." 8 June 2003, http://smith.hanover.edu/sqwyatt.html.
Study prompts for Wyatt's poetry including "The Long Love," "Whoso List to Hunt," "They Flee From Me," and "Mine Own John Poins." Keyed to the *Longman Anthology of British Literature*, 2d ed.

"Selected Poetry of Sir Thomas Wyatt (1503–1542)." *Representative Poetry Online*. 8 June 2003, http://eir.library.utoronto.ca/rpo/display/poet367.html.
  The full text of a selection of Wyatt's poems including: "Mine own John Poins," "Whoso List to Hunt," and "They flee from me."

"Thomas Wyatt." *Poets.org*. 8 June 2003, http://www.poets.org/poets/poets. cfm?prmID=329.
  A biography of Wyatt.

"Wyatt and Surrey." *Bartleby.com*. 8 June 2003, http://www.bartleby.com/ 213/1307.html.
  An entry on the poetics of Wyatt and Surrey from *The Cambridge History of English and American Literature,* 1907–1921

Biographies and Criticism

Caldwell, Ellen, C. "Sir Thomas Wyatt." Richardson, *Sixteenth-Century British Nondramatic Writers, 1st ser.* (Dictionary of Literary Biography 132), 346–363.

Foley, Stephen Merriam. *Sir Thomas Wyatt*. Boston: Twayne, 1990.

Heale, Elizabeth. *Wyatt, Surrey, and Early Tudor Poetry*. London and New York: Longman, 1998.

"Sir Thomas Wyatt." *Poetry Criticism* 27: 298–377.
  Excerpts of comments and criticism on Wyatt from 1963–1993, with an annotated bibliography.

"Thomas Wyatt." *Literature Criticism from 1400 to 1800* 70: 216–380.
  Excerpts of comments and criticism on Wyatt from 1557–1999.

Bibliographies

Hulse, Clark. "Thomas Wyatt the Elder." Hager, *Major Tudor Authors*, 476–484.
  Brief biography, survey of major works and themes, critical reception, and bibliography of works by and about Wyatt.

Jentoft, Clyde W. *Sir Thomas Wyatt and Henry Howard, Earl of Surrey: A Reference Guide*. Boston: Hall, 1980.

Chronological List of Authors

c. 1422–1491, Caxton, William
1460?–1529, Skelton, John
c. 1475–1511, Hawes, Stephen
1475?–1522, Douglas, Gavin
1475?–1552, Barclay, Alexander
1477?–1535, More, Sir Thomas
c. 1486–1555, Lindsay, Sir David
c. 1490–1546, Elyot, Sir Thomas
1491–1547, Henry VIII
c. 1495–1536, Tyndale, William
1495–1563, Bale, John
1497?–1580?, Heywood, John
1503–1542, Wyatt, Sir Thomas
c. 1505–1556, Udall, Nicholas
c. 1506–1552, Leland, John
1515/16–1568, Ascham, Roger
1516–1587, Foxe, John
1517?–1547, Howard, Henry, Earl of
    Surrey
1521–1546, Askew, Anne
c. 1523–1581, Wilson, Thomas
c. 1529–1591, Puttenham, George
1530–1566, Hoby, Thomas
c. 1531–1611, Mulcaster, Richard
1532–1584, Norton, Thomas
1533–1603, Elizabeth I
c. 1534–1577, Gascoigne, George
1536?–1605?, Golding, Arthur
1536–1608, Sackville, Thomas, First Earl
    of Dorset, Baron Buckhurst
1542–1587, Mary, Queen of Scots
c. 1550–1631, Harvey, Gabriel
1551–1623, Camden, William
c. 1552–1599, Spenser, Edmund
1552–1616, Hakluyt, Richard
c. 1553–1625, Florio, John
1554–1586, Sidney, Sir Philip
1554?–1600, Hooker, Richard
1554?–1606, Lyly, John
1554–1618, Ralegh [Raleigh], Sir Walter
1554–1628, Greville, Fulke, First Baron
    Brooke

1555–1626, Andrewes, Lancelot
1555?–1626, Breton, Nicholas
1556–1596, Peele, George
1558–1592, Greene, Robert
1558–1594, Kyd, Thomas
1558–1625, Lodge, Thomas
1559?–1634, Chapman, George
1560?–1600, Deloney, Thomas
1560–1612, Harington, Sir John
1560–1633, Munday, Anthony
1561?–1595, Southwell, Saint Robert
1561–1626, Bacon, Francis
1562?—1619, Daniel, Samuel
1562–1621, Herbert, Mary (Sidney),
    Countess of Pembroke
1563–1631, Drayton, Michael
1564–1593, Marlowe, Christopher
1564–1616, Shakespeare, William
1566–1625, James I (James VI of
    Scotland)
fl. 1567–c. 1573, Whitney, Isabella
1567–1601, Nashe, Thomas
1567–1620, Campion, Thomas
1568–1639, Wotton, Sir Henry
1569–1626, Davies, John
1569–1645, Lanyer, Aemilia
1572–1631, Donne, John
1572?–1632, Dekker, Thomas
1572/3–1637, Jonson, Ben
1574–1627, Barnfield, Richard
1574?–1641, Heywood, Thomas
1574–1656, Hall, Joseph
1575?–1626, Tourneur, Cyril
1576–1634, Marston, John
1577–1640, Burton, Robert
c. 1578–c. 1626, Webster, John
1578–1644, Sandys, George
1579–1625, Fletcher, John
1580–1627, Middleton, Thomas
1580–1631, Smith, Captain John
1580–1653, Taylor, John
1582–1635, Corbett, Richard

1582–1648, Herbert, Edward, of
    Cherbury
1582–1650, Fletcher, Phineas
1583–1640, Massinger, Philip
1584–1616, Beaumont, Francis
1585?–1623, Fletcher, Giles, the Younger
1585?–1626, Rowley, William
1585–1639, Cary, Elizabeth, Lady
1585–1649, Drummond, William, of
    Hawthornden
1586–after 1639, Ford, John
1587–1651?, Wroth, Mary, Lady
1588–1667, Wither, George
1588–1679, Hobbes, Thomas
1590?–1645?, Browne, William, of
    Tavistock
c. 1590–1652/3, Brome, Richard
1591–1674, Herrick, Robert
1592–1644, Quarles, Francis
1592–1669, King, Henry
1593–1633, Herbert, George
1593–1683, Walton, Izaak
1594/5–1640, Carew, Thomas
1596–1666, Shirley, James
1600–1645, Strode, William
1600–1649, Charles I
1601?–1665, Earle, John
1605–1635, Randolph, Thomas
1605–1654, Habington, William

1605–1682, Browne, Sir Thomas
1606–1668, D'Avenant, William
1606–1687, Waller, Edmund
1608–1661, Fuller, Thomas
1608–1674, Milton, John
1609–1642, Suckling, Sir John
1611–1677, Harrington, James
1612/13–1649, Crashaw, Richard
1613–1658, Cleveland, John
1613–1667, Taylor, Jeremy
1613–1680, Butler, Samuel
1614–1687, More, Henry
1615–1669, Denham, John
1615–1691, Baxter, Richard
1616–1704, L'Estrange, Roger
1618–1657/8, Lovelace, Richard
1618–1667, Cowley, Abraham
1620–1706, Evelyn, John
1621–1678, Marvell, Andrew
1621–1695, Vaughan, Henry
1623–1723, Cavendish, Margaret
    (Lucas), Duchess of Newcastle
1624–1704, Lead, Jane Ward
1627–1691, Boyle, Robert
1628–1688, Bunyan, John
1631–1664, Philips, Katherine
1638–1706, Sackville, Charles, Lord
    Buckhurst, Sixth Earl of Dorset
fl. 1654–1660, Trapnel, Anna

Author Index

About the Author

STEVEN K. GALBRAITH is Ph.D. candidate in English Renaissance Literature at Ohio State University. Before returning to school he worked as a reference librarian at the University of Maine.